Peak Performance in 60 Seconds

If you go to work and have lots of stress to deal with and would like more physical energy, mental sharpness and emotional balance then this book is for you!

Peak Performance in 60 Seconds

The 4 Essentials to Maximise Your Energy, Resilience and Performance

Chris Walton MSc

AWAKEN
BOOKS

First published in 2011 by Awaken Books.
Awaken Books, 26 Kelvedon Road, Fulham,
London SW6 5BW

ISBN 978-0-9565527-1-6

British Library of Cataloguing in Publication Data.
A catalogue record for this book is available from the
British Library.

Charts and book text styling:
Bernard Chandler www.graffik.co.uk

Printed in the UK by Lightning Source

Contents

Introduction

You can read and apply this book
In less than 60 minutes.

I N TODAY'S FAST-PACED WORLD of competitive workplaces and relentless change, increasing your energy and resilience is essential to be able to perform at your best. This book shows you the most advanced and effective way to maximise your energy, resilience and mental and emotional fitness. You will learn a practical 10 step plan that you can apply immediately.

In Chapters 1-4 **Managing your Mind**, the new understanding of the power of your belief systems on your health, performance and success is explained. This is essential empowering knowledge that we all need to understand. You learn the different effects the conscious and subconscious mind has on your performance and I teach you **The Gamma Brain Technique©**.

The Gamma Brain Technique is scientifically validated to create a 'super focused mind state' and activate the 'genius centres' of the brain in just 60 seconds. This technique is the most advanced and effective way to achieve a heightened state of awareness, concentration and focused attention. It is ideal to use before meetings, presentations, pitches, important/ difficult conversations, to become calm, centred and present and to program your subconscious mind with your professional and personal goals. The technique is also used for problem solving and as a rest and renewal mediation. Brain activity has been measured when using The Gamma Brain Technique (and validated by brain surgeon and Professor of Neurosurgery, Kazadi Kalangu M.D. – Vice President of the World Federation of Neurosurgical Societies). This technique creates the premium brain state and the more you use it, the more you are literally training yourself for peak performance states of mind know as Flow or The Zone.

In Chapters 5 & 6 **Managing your Emotions**, you learn that most of your emotional reactions are based on past experience associations stored in your subconscious mind. Think about it, if you were consciously choosing your emotions surely you would choose to feel calm, relaxed or some form of good all the time, but you can't!

Our emotional brain is one million times more active than our thinking brain, and this means that measuring, understanding and developing your emotional intelligence is absolutely essential to increase your energy, resilience and performance. You cannot become more resilient is your choices to current situations are based on emotional reactions from past experiences and associations. This is just one reason most people find change hard; emotions keep you fixed on a certain 'bandwidth' of behaviours and responses available to you. I show you how to change this 'bandwidth' and how to eliminate worry, doubt, fear, anxiety and any other psychological and emotional stress using the scientifically validated Emotional Balance Technique©. You can take the Individual Effectiveness™ profile which measures 16 key areas of emotional intelligence and then develop a set of practices and techniques to improve your self-awareness, self-management and your awareness and management of others.

In Chapter 7, **Managing your Fuel**, you learn the two most important physiological rules you have to follow with your nutrition to maximise your physical energy. You learn a simple 'post meal and snack test' to help you maintain a high performance rate.

Chapter 8, **Managing your Body**, explains that human beings do not work like computers doing more and more, faster and faster, running multiple programs for long periods of time in a continual linear progression. Our bodies work in 90 minutes cycles of high output and focus followed by a need for renewal and recovery. Learning how to work with these cycles stops fatigue and burn out and boosts your energy and resilience on all levels, enhancing your creativity, productivity and performance.

Chapter 9 summarises **The 10 steps to maximise your energy, resilience and performance** and you can **start** the **30 day challenge**.

Get your free video training course at www.ChrisWaltonUK.com

58 minutes left. Are you ready? Let's go...

Part 1

Managing Your Mind

Chapter 1

Using Your Mind to Maximise Your Energy, Resilience and Performance

YOUR MIND IS THE STOREHOUSE for your beliefs, feelings and thoughts and learning how to manage it is one of the most important and powerful things you can ever do to be successful in your professional and personal life.

Many years ago we used to think the mind was just a function of the brain. Today we understand that the mind is an information field that interpenetrates every cell of the brain and body connecting everything together like a huge information network. Our beliefs, feelings and thoughts transfer themselves into electrical-chemical impulses that communicate with and affect every cell in the body (**see Fig 1.0**). Every thought and feeling you have, whether it is feeling anxious, confident, doubtful motivated, stressed or energised is known by your whole body from the top of your head to the tip of your toe. The mind and body are one integrated system. Learning how to 'program' your mind is the first place to start in order to increase your energy, resilience and performance. To do this you must understand the power of your conscious and subconscious beliefs.

■ ■ ■

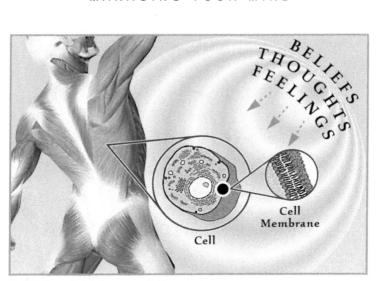

Fig 1.0: Our mind is in every cell of our body

Your Beliefs Control Your Thoughts, Feelings and Actions

Your belief systems are the most powerful force in your mind and body and the most influential key to maximising performance and success. Unfortunately most of what we do and say is driven by beliefs that we may not ever have examined, let alone agreed to hold as true. What is it that makes you think, feel and act the way you do? The iceberg model illustrated in **Fig 1.1** provides a simple metaphor that explains how beliefs influence our emotions and motivate our actions. As you know, an iceberg is approximately 90% unseen, submerged underwater, so we see only the tip of it. We can't really know how big it is or what it looks like. That iceberg is very much like beliefs - very few of them are conscious (above the water line of our knowing). Most remain hidden from us, submerged deep in our subconscious minds. We are not aware of what our subconscious assumptions and beliefs actually are, and yet they influence every aspect of our lives.

7

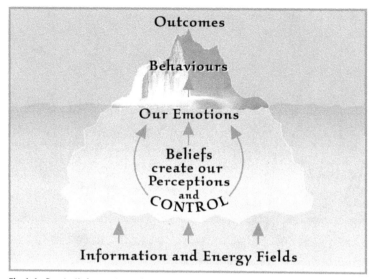

Fig 1.1: Our beliefs create and control our perceptions. The way we perceive the world drives our emotional responses to events and interactions, which in turn governs the actions we take and, ultimately, has a large effect on the outcome of events and interactions.

For now you can ignore the reference in the illustration to information and energy fields. We'll explore those in a later chapter. Just to be absolutely clear in our terminology - our behaviours are our actions (what we do, say, etc.) and how we carry those actions out. Behaviours have a style that are encoded by beliefs, for instance by our worldview and our personal style, which are things that can be generalised into 'types' (or even stereotypes). So, for example, some people are conservative, others liberal. Some are Type A personalities (outgoing, action-oriented, extroverted) and some Type B (more retiring, introspective and introverted). Obviously what we do and say – and how we do and say things – strongly influences the outcomes of our interactions and the situations we create in our lives.

Our behaviours are driven by our emotions and feelings. We all know how powerful emotions can be, they can inspire us or paralyse us. When we feel confident, excited, appreciative, happy and full of vitality, we think, behave and perform very differently from when we feel self-conscious, unsure, frustrated, stressed, tired or depressed. What we might not be aware of, however, is that many of the emotions we feel are determined by a deeper level of cause-and-effect – the level of our perceptions and beliefs. For example, if you express your opinion to someone and that person disagrees with you, you could feel many different emotions in response. You could simply accept that person has a different viewpoint and not feel much at all, because your underlying belief may be that everyone is entitled to his or her opinion. You could feel surprised that the person disagrees, and perhaps then feel frustrated that perhaps you were misheard. Your underlying belief is that the person is like you in many other respects and so should think like you. You might even feel self-righteous, feeling yours is the correct and logical opinion, and also feel dismissive of that person, thinking him or her ignorant or misguided. An underlying belief driving that response might be that there is a moral imperative behind the opinion and that any smart or ethical person would believe as you do. There are many possible responses because there are a myriad of beliefs that drive your emotional self. The point here is that to maximise your performance we need to go deeper than positive thinking and motivation trainings and techniques – you need to get to the level of your beliefs. Emotions can be clues to your beliefs, but they are not enough in and of themselves to tell us what is really influencing you and your potential.

Beliefs are Not Attitudes

It is important to understand that I am not talking about attitudes here. Our overall emotional template and thought processes are more than a set of attitudes. Attitudes, as in a positive versus a negative outlook on facing challenges and meeting opportunities, are important, but they are still surface level in terms of the impact they have on our performance, and they are subject to situation, environment, the people around us, and other transient influences. Beliefs go much deeper and form a more or less stable, even if subconscious, 'palette' by which we live our lives. The reality is that percolating beneath any of our core emotions and thoughts is a set of conscious and subconscious beliefs that control our perceptions of life and thus also control our emotions, thoughts, and the quality of our actions and behaviours and therefore our performance. The beliefs are the scaffolding that holds our emotions and thoughts in place, however transient those emotions and thoughts may be. Our beliefs are the foundation upon which rests the entire structure of our life and its perceived quality.

Building on the definitions I have just given, I can go one step further and define belief as:

> A belief is a thought or a collection of thoughts that determines a person's perceptions of the world and so influences, and even dictates, the choices that person makes, the relationships he/she has, the behaviours he/she demonstrates and ultimately their accomplishments, success, performance and quality of life that person lives.

Beliefs are Not Just Psychological

Beliefs are not only abstract things that impact you psychologically and behaviourally. They exist in the form of thought patterns in your physical being. They are very real electro chemical signals that are broadcast throughout every cell of your body. They impact every aspect of your being, from your 'happiness factor' to the strength of your immune system, from your outlook on life to the cascade of your hormones, enzymes and overall body chemistry. Thoughts are things. And beliefs are the content and substance of those thoughts. As Dr Herbert Benson, pioneer of mind-body medicine, has said, after decades of research at Harvard Medical School and other places,

> *"We should not ignore compelling brain research that demon-strates that beliefs manifest themselves throughout our bodies."*

To really maximise your performance you don't have to change your thoughts, you have to change and update your beliefs.

A startling fact is that most of our beliefs are subconscious. They drive our behaviour, control our performance and colour our life without us even knowing how or why. We all know people who may not be very talented or qualified or whatever, but they are stellar at advocating for themselves and often win opportunities that we thought others might have better deserved. Are they just lucky or charmed? What do they have that so works to their advantage? The answer is not their positive attitude, but their underlying beliefs about themselves and the world. All those qualities we associate with a person's 'personality' are really the constellation of their core beliefs emerging as attitudes, emotions, actions, skills, gifts, and so on. Add up all of the small and large, simplistic and complex, conscious and subconscious beliefs that you hold and that are driving your behaviour and personality at every moment of every day and you get a sense of just how important your beliefs are in unleashing your potential.

We screen our experiences according to our beliefs, focusing on what our beliefs tell us is important and ignoring or glossing over the rest. We tend to filter the world for information that supports our belief system; conversely, we filter out that which contradicts it.

Where Do Your Beliefs Come From?

The way we form beliefs involves a host of influences that are working on us from before our birth. As children we depend on others to teach us about the way the world is. We learn a specific language, which in and of itself structures what we are even capable of conceiving and believing. For example, some languages have no words with which to talk about the future, focusing only on the past or the present. Imagine how different such a world is from your own. You also may have been raised with a particular religion or family politics, or with a specific family attitude about the value of science, art, logic, and creativity. You were raised to expect a certain type of emotional expressiveness, perhaps in a family that did not hug or touch much, which coloured the way you view relationships, intimacy, and so on. The fact is that we are exposed to a myriad of ways, both blatant and subtle, to filter the world. You were taught what to include and ignore, what to value and devalue, and on and on.

For most of us, our early years are ones in which we didn't think for ourselves at all or very much; we simply accepted what we were told and formed beliefs based on what those around us believed. That's all well and good. Children after all have to learn some way and from someone. But as adults, we find that running a version of the same belief programme we learned as children no longer aids our potential. So, it pays to become conscious of all the ways we form our beliefs in the first place.

■ ■ ■

THE MAJORITY OF OUR BELIEFS CAME FROM:
Parents/Family, Friends/Colleagues/Peers, Schools, Religion, Media, Social-Economic Class, Geographical Location, Culture, History, Science, Politics and so on.

The truth is that, as Albert Einstein once said, *"Common sense is the collection of prejudices acquired by the age of eighteen."* And that is the problem, we take all those beliefs – many of which are out-dated and limiting into our adulthood unquestioned and uninvestigated. We inherit so many of our beliefs at such a deeply subconscious level that they still control our choices and actions today, even when the choices and actions of yesterday are making our todays unproductive and potentially sabotaging our performance and success.

To maximise your performance it is essential to update and reprogram your belief systems about who you are, what your potential is and what you can achieve. Due to advances in our knowledge of the mind-body connection and a branch of psychology called 'energy psychology' (more on this later) it is possible to do so, without years of talk therapy or involved self-analysis. Logic holds no sway over the subconscious, which is why our positive thinking, good intentions and New Year's resolutions so often fail. The door to the subconscious is through the body, as I will soon show you.

The key point here is that your beliefs are in every cell of your body and control your perceptions of everything in your life. They precede and drive your emotional reactions, thought processes, the quality of your actions and determine the level of success and performance you can achieve. To maximise your performance and success you have to have empowering goal specific beliefs programmed into your subconscious mind. You want your subconscious mind working for you not against you.

Changing Beliefs Increases Sales by 50%

Skill, Experience, Knowledge, Motivation, Belief. What's the problem? Some years ago I worked with a large advertising company who had invested £5million in moving from selling just hard copy advertising to offering a full portfolio of internet advertising options. Within 3 months of the new services launch, the sales figures were well below target. The sales teams were seasoned sales professionals that were used to hitting target and enjoying their bonus. They had received the new product training, which was quite straight forward, yet the sales figures were getting worse. I was called in to see if it was a motivation issue. It wasn't a motivation issue, but it was a belief issue! The bottom line was the sales teams and sales managers (and interestingly some of the directors) didn't believe deep down that the market was ready for the product. This led to the sales teams not leaving enough time in their meetings and pitches to offer the new services and hence very low sales. I ran a belief change training programme for their 12 UK offices and within six weeks of ending the programme there was a 50% increase in sales. Beliefs drive everything we do!

The Power of Belief and Your Physical Health

To really drive home the power of our beliefs not just on performance but on our physical body here is one amazing true story:

Mr Wright had just hours to live. He had tumours the size of oranges throughout his body, his lungs were filled with fluid, his spleen and liver were enormously swollen, and he couldn't breathe without the help of supplemental oxygen. His physician, Dr Klopfer, had done everything he could use standard medical therapies to try to help Mr Wright – to no avail.

Now that the end seemed near, Mr Wright was willing to consider non-standard treatments. One of these was a cancer drug, called Krebiozen, which, even though it was still undergoing clinical research, was being hailed by the popular media as a possible wonder cure for cancer. Dr Klopfer had access to the still-experimental drug, and when Mr Wright begged to be allowed to try it, Dr Klopfer agreed, even though doing so would go against medical protocol. He gained access to the drug and administered it to Mr Wright on a Friday, and then he left the hospital for the weekend, believing that Mr Wright would be dead by the time he returned on Monday. But when Monday came, Dr Klopfer was shocked to see Mr Wright up and walking around the ward, as if he had never been at death's door. Tests were run, and the results were stunning – the tumours had shrunk to half their original size. Dr Klopfer continued the Krebiozen treatments, and in less than two weeks Mr Wright was tumour free. Soon he was released from the hospital, returning home a healthy man. A couple of months later, the media reported on the preliminary results of the clinical trials of this supposed wonder drug. The verdict: Krebiozen did not appear to be effective against cancer. Mr Wright heard these reports, and soon thereafter he felt unwell again. Examination revealed that his tumours were back. As his health deteriorated, he was re-admitted to the hospital. Dr Klopfer was at a loss to explain what was happening with Mr Wright. The dramatic disappearance of the tumours and their reappearance seemed to be more than a remission and relapse. He suspected that somehow Mr Wright's beliefs were involved, and that, in fact, those beliefs might be the strongest factor in what was happening. To test this theory, he gave Mr Wright injections of sterile water but told him that it was a 'new double-strength version' of the wonder drug Krebiozen. Again, Mr Wright's tumours melted away, he regained his health, was released from the hospital and resumed his normal life. Shortly thereafter, there was a lot of press about an official report from the American Medical Association, the most respected and recognised medical professional organisation in the United States, declaring unequivocally that Krebiozen didn't work. In fact, one headline declared, 'Nationwide Tests Show Krebiozen to Be a Worthless Drug in the Treatment of Cancer'. Upon hearing this news, Mr Wright felt devastated, and, sure enough, a short time later his tumours reappeared and his health declined precipitously. He died two days after being readmitted to the hospital. Dr Klopfer published a paper in a medical journal about his experience with Mr Wright, concluding that Mr Wright's optimistic beliefs appeared to be the main factor in the disappearance of his tumours and the regaining of his health, and the loss of that optimism and belief the main factor in their reappearance and Mr Wright's death.

As this true story demonstrates, our beliefs are exceptionally powerful. And their power is pervasive, affecting us at every level of our being – from our moment-by-moment feelings about ourselves, to what we think we can achieve and accomplish, to what we expect to receive from those around us and to our perception of the state of the world at large. Our personal lives conform to our beliefs, and our world reflects back to us our collective beliefs. In fact, our thoughts and beliefs are so important to the state of our overall well-being that they are the object not only of psychological study but also of physiological, sports performance, medical and biological research. As leading neuroscientist at the University of Pennsylvania Dr Andrew Newberg says,

"I have come to realise that the study of beliefs may be the single most important quest, both scientifically and spiritually."

We simply cannot create lasting change and express more of our potential without updating and changing our beliefs. In Chapter 2 I show you exactly why will power, motivational techniques and positive thinking hardly ever create lasting change.

■ ■ ■

Chapter 2

How to Move from Motivation to Lasting Change

M OST MIND-SET motivation and behaviour change training programmes often don't work or are short lived. Why? The answer lies in the two separate departments of your mind. We have two minds: the conscious mind and the subconscious mind. I've mentioned the subconscious a little already, and it's time now to dive into this fascinating reality in more detail as we will see the huge impact the subconscious has on performance and success.

Your conscious mind is your thinking mind and is associated with your personal identity. It is involved in creativity, logic, reasoning, some decision-making, will-power and positive thinking. Your subconscious mind controls your automatic bodily functions and is the storehouse for your beliefs and emotional reactions, learned habits and actions, judgements and memory (see Fig 2.0). Aligning both minds is a fundamental key for maximising performance, let's see why that is.

Your Mind Was Programmed Long Ago

From midway through our gestation as foetuses into child-hood and beyond, our life experiences are recorded and stored in the subconscious mind. Every single thing that has ever happened to you and been said to you is recorded in your subconscious mind. These early experiences and the influx of new information we experience throughout childhood combine to create our beliefs, which determine 'the rules' that shape the way we create everything in our lives, from our personal relationships to our professions, and our decisions about our future.

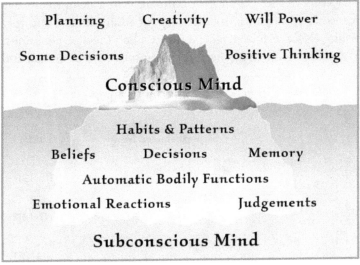

Fig 2.0: The different functions of the conscious and subconscious mind.

Figure 2.1 illustrates just how much of our subconscious is open to 'programming', to use a computer metaphor, by outside influences, such as our parents, teachers, culture and more. The process is quite fascinating, as it is aligned with brain wave activity. We have five levels of brainwave activity: gamma, beta, alpha, theta and delta. The gamma wave creates heightened awareness and a super focused mind state. (Using the Gamma Brain Technique you will achieve this in 60 seconds.)

Beta brain waves kick in when we have a very busy mind, perhaps feeling stressed and juggling activities. When the brain is in the alpha state, the body is relaxed and the two hemispheres of the brain are more coherent. This creates increased whole-brain functioning leading to heightened levels of intuition, creativity, logic, wisdom and insight. Theta waves are associated with states of deep meditation, trance and light sleep. Delta waves arise mostly during deep sleep. For the first two years of life, we are predominantly in a delta brainwave pattern. Although this is deep sleep for adults, infants and very young children produce delta waves when they are conscious. They are downloading massive amounts of environmental and

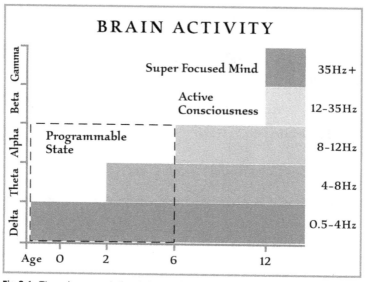

Fig 2.1: There is a correlation between brainwave activity and how we download the 'rules of life' during our first six years. Adapted from the original work of Dr Bruce Lipton and used with kind permission.

emotional data, soaking up the world through their five senses and recording and storing it in their subconscious minds for later use.

From about the ages of two to six years, our brains switch to a predominantly theta brainwave state, which represents a state of dreaminess and contemplation. This is when many children develop imaginary worlds, as they mix up their external and interior worlds.

After about age six, we exist mostly in the alpha brain wave range, until we reach about age twelve, when beta waves predominate. These states coincide with the start of senior school, where logic and reason become our primary mode of learning and processing information.

From midway through pregnancy and the first six years of life, a child is in a highly programmable brainwave state. This has been found to be a 'super learning' state. It is why young children can absorb huge amounts of information and can be taught so easily. For example, they can almost effortlessly become fluent in several languages at the same time if they are exposed to them on a daily basis. In these formative years, a child does not have to be specifically shown and coached by his or her parents to learn behaviours - information is learned and behaviours adopted simply by exposure and observation. This early programming also includes downloading the core information and opinions that form the essence of our feelings of self-worth and of our perceived gifts and abilities. During this time we lay down the foundation of our social self and are fundamental style of our social and interpersonal interactions.

So, whereas consciously you may feel and think that you are in charge of the quality, direction and success of your life, the truth is that at a subconscious level you may be simply living out adapted patterns and programs that you learned from others during your childhood. As an adult these patterns may be causing conflict or resistance toward achieving success and peak performance.

Your subconscious software is like the software that runs on your computer. You may have loaded many software programs when you first got your computer, and now, many years later, you may be using only a few of them. However, the unused programs are still there, running in the background, using electricity, energy and resources. Your subconscious beliefs and emotional reactions do the same – they run without you being aware of them, often depleting your inner resources, putting stress of your nervous system reducing your potential and subtly leading you in a way that is not in line with your conscious goals. This is why it is essential that as an adult you become aware of your subconscious programs, update them, and align them with your conscious goals and desires. When you do, you have a much greater chance of performing at your best because your subconscious mind holds an enormous amount of power. It is power you have at your disposal, to use to your benefit. Let's now explore just how much power and potential you have stored inside you, awaiting to be unleashed.

The Power of Your Subconscious Mind

The conscious and subconscious minds can be likened to infor-mation processors, each being able to process a certain amount of information. Think of each as having a certain bandwidth of processing power that can be measured in bits per second (bps).

Just compare the difference in processing power between the two departments of the mind; the conscious mind processes 40 bits per second but staggeringly the processing power of the subconscious mind is a whopping 40,000,000 bits per second.

Fig 2.2: This image contains at least 40 million 'bits of information', each called a pixel. In one second your subconscious would 'download' the whole image which would mean approximately forty million neural impulses taking place in your brain every second. Of these forty million, you become conscious of only about 40 of these bits of information, which then make up your conscious potential. The rest are processed at the subconscious level.
There is a lot more going on inside of you than you are aware of!

The *subconscious mind has one million times* more processing power than the conscious mind and this makes it a huge factor in maximising your potential and performance of any kind. As a visual metaphor to help you grasp the differences in processing power of the two minds, take a look at **Fig 2.2**, which shows the British Houses of Parliament and the famous clock tower Big Ben. Imagine that every pixel in the image is a bit of data converted into information inside your brain. Let's say that the image has 40 million pixels or bits of data. Your subconscious mind would download the whole image in one second. Now what you would become consciously aware of is a different matter entirely. In the same second what would bubble up to your conscious awareness is shown in **Fig 2.3**.

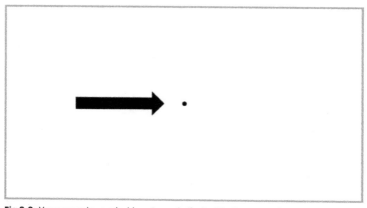

Fig 2.3: Your conscious mind is extremely limited in its processing capacity, which is about one million times less than the processing capacity of your subconscious mind. Not much is it?

How Conscious are You?

What percentage of your day-to-day thoughts, feelings and actions come from your conscious choices as compared to those that are learned programs and behaviours coming from your subconscious mind? Astonishingly 95% to 99% of all your thoughts, feelings and actions each day are governed by learned programs in your subconscious mind. Almost everything that you think and do in life is driven from a level of mind you are not aware of! (**See Fig 2.4**).

Which part of our mind does positive thinking come from? You got it - the conscious mind with its 40 bits per second processor operating a maximum of 5% of the day. Now it is quite easy to see why most change and motivational programs are short lived.

As an example of our subconscious programming; once we learn how to do something well, we don't have to consciously work to carry out that action. If you drive, you've probably experienced arriving at your destination and realising you were

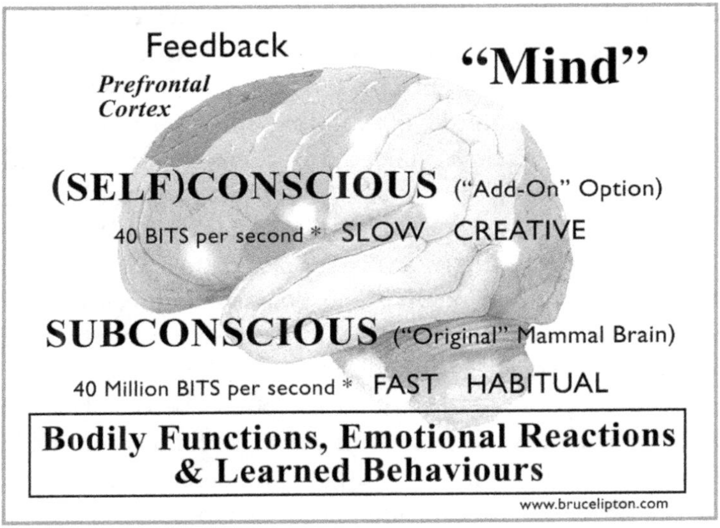

Fig 2.4: Adapted from the original work of Dr Bruce Lipton and used with his kind permission. The subconscious mind is correlated to the aspects of the brain to do with survival, bodily functions, learned emotional reactions and autopilot behaviours. The conscious mind is correlated to the most evolved part of our brain-the prefrontal cortex. Dr Lipton humorously says that being (self) conscious is an 'Add-On' option as most people live their life mostly unconsciously, due to the huge difference in processing power.

not very aware of having made the journey. Having learned and 'downloaded' the driving program, you only have to have the intent and the program plays without any conscious awareness required. Riding a bike, getting dressed, checking email, cooking a favourite meal – many of the activities that fill our lives have become rote-learned subconscious programs. Many of these subconscious and rote programs are essential, as we cannot think consciously about more than a couple of things at the same time. In an ideal world, everyone would be aware of all of their behaviours, actions, and thoughts; however, in the fast-paced modern world, this is simply an impossibility – and it may have always been so, since we are capable of processing so much information that we don't need on a moment to moment basis. We have to screen out some of these streams of information so as not to be overwhelmed. However, the downside of our lack of awareness is that although the conscious mind can be incredibly creative and innovative, it can also be incredibly demanding and busy. It flits from one thought to another very quickly, and that can be a recipe for inefficiency, diversion and the many excuses that keep us from living up to our potential and realising our goals. In addition, most of us grow comfortable with those we see on a regular basis and our interactions become rote. As their behaviours and emotional responses become familiar and predictable, so do ours. This can make for a comfortable existence without too many surprises to 'upset the applecart' of our lives. But it can also mean that our performance, marriage, friendships, work and other relationships suffer from comfort zones, neglect and boredom.

You might be surprised at just how unruly your conscious mind is and how rote you have become in your interactions with others. As a test, pay attention over the next few hours –and if you can remember to, over the next few days – to the thoughts that flit through your mind. You might just be appalled at how easily distracted your conscious mind gets and how often you are acting from rote programming, almost robotically. You may also find that if you start to observe your inner voice you will realise it never stops. It is constantly on the go talking about past experiences or future events.

There are many kinds of awareness techniques you can practice to return to 'in the moment awareness' – to aim to stop playing back these potentially limiting rote behaviours and responses. Try a few of these and see how they work for you. They can provide clues to how you are thinking, feeling and acting at a subconscious level.

Expanding your Conscious Awareness Exercises:

1. For just 60 seconds breathe in and out through your nose. Focus on feeling your breath going into your nose and expanding your belly. See if you can count how many breaths you take in that one minute without your mind wandering onto other thoughts. It sounds easy, you may be surprised how little conscious mind control you have.

2. When in conversation with someone, aim to be truly present to that person and listen to what he or she is saying. There are generally two types of listening: The first type is to listen with the intent to reply, which naturally is what most of us do. We have already formulated our answers or next part of the conversation before we have truly listened to the other person. The second type of listening is listening with the intent to truly understand the other person's point of view and situation. So in your next conversation really intend to listen and understand the person before you reply. Be as present and conscious as you can.

3. Use the STOP model to increase your conscious awareness as much as you can throughout the day. STOP stands for; **STOP – THINK – OPTIONS – PROCEED**. It is a simple model to help you make conscious decisions and act from the present moment with wisdom and clarity rather than reacting from autopilot programming. Get into the habit throughout the day of asking yourself, 'Am I conscious now'. Remember the more you can increase your consciousness the more choice you have.

■ ■ ■

> **MAXIMISE YOUR ENERGY, RESILIENCE AND PERFORMANCE ACTION STEP 1:**
> Every day in every conversation be consciously aware. Use the STOP model. Be as present and in the moment as you can. Make your choices and responses from a conscious place.

Being more conscious on a daily basis and making time for self-reflection and quieting the mind are life transforming practices.

By now hopefully it is clear that when your conscious mind is busy thinking about past experiences or future intentions and desires, your subconscious is also at work, driving the behaviours that you show to the world. These behaviours may seem like you are consciously choosing them but actually that is an illusion as they are driven from the subconscious. It is mostly your subconscious that is dictating your performance and success. As brain researcher Rita Carter explains in *The Brain Book:*

> *"Your brain registers events via the sense organs almost imme-diately, but it takes up to half a second to become conscious of them. In order to generate effective responses in a fast changing environment, the brain therefore plans and executes moment by moment actions unconsciously."*

It is very important to understand, however, that the sub-conscious mind is fairly straightforward – it is mainly a stimulus and response system, what is programmed in is what comes out. Have you ever had an experience where someone 'pushed your buttons'? When someone said something to you that created an automatic emotional reaction? Maybe your boss or colleague? It is not what that person said or did, especially if you just met that person. It is how it was said including the body language and facial expressions that may have stirred subconscious associations to memories within you, those past programs you are running automatically. It is from those subconscious memories that your actions and responses arise, and remember that a minimum of 95% of the time we are doing this. In effect we are robots, prisoners of our personal and cultural beliefs and conditioning. Being resilient to change and performing at your best cannot happen until you make the choice to break free from this and claim your mind back. Massive amounts of our mental and emotional energy are used up daily by unconscious reactions. Living unconsciously doesn't bode well for creative and innovative thought. It is the most severe barrier to us expressing our potential and maximising our performance.

Take a moment now to think through situations at work and in your personal life where you have these automatic emotional reactions. Who 'pushes your buttons'? Who and what do you react to that makes you angry, frustrated, stressed or anxious?

Reach New Levels of Performance using the Power of Your Subconscious Mind

To increase your energy, resilience, performance, to make the best conscious decisions you can and to optimise your whole brain and body functioning it is absolutely essential that you have your subconscious mind up to date and in alignment with your conscious goals. If you don't, you are treating your mind in ways you probably do not even treat your computer. Would you run your computer on software that is decades old? Would you put up with the resulting limitations and inefficiencies? Would you be content to be unable to access the latest and greatest applications because the software won't recognise it or interface with it? I don't think anyone reading this book would. So, the question arises, why are you content to be running out-dated, limiting and inefficient internal programs – the programs of your subconscious mind?

Your subconscious mind is a 40-million-bit processor that operates at least 95% of the time whereas your conscious mind is a 40-bit processor that operates only about 5% of the time. When you update and reprogram your subconscious mind to be in alignment with your conscious goals, you utilise this vast processing power to efficiently make connections between your subconscious and conscious mind. Once the link is established, you bring more of your brain power to fruition to achieving your best in every situation.

To use another analogy, think of a pilot flying an airliner from London to New York. The pilot can expend enormous energy doing everything himself – such as managing trajectory, altitude, velocity, and such – or he can program the plane's autopilot with the destination data and let the plane fly itself. Being able to trust your subconscious as your autopilot can free you in ways you can barely now imagine. As leading neuro-scientist Dr Joe Dispenza explains in his ground-breaking book, Evolve Your Brain,

> *"When you unify your conscious and subconscious minds then you have access to greater potential."*

One of the reasons why your subconscious will filter your experiences to make links and associations only to things that have been programmed into it as being relevant to you. Have you ever been at a party and been fully engaged in a conversation and from a distant part of the room you hear your name? Although you may have been fully engrossed in your conversation, your subconscious mind with its forty-million-bit-per-second information processor heard your name and brought it to your conscious awareness for you to decide whether you needed to take any action or not.

Updating out-dated, self-sabotaging 'programmes' with new, self-supportive ones, such as those found in the appendix at the back of this book using the Gamma Brain Technique and the Emotional Balance Technique will dramatically improve your mental clarity, emotional balance, physical energy and performance. The likelihood of achieving goals and performing at your best is astronomically higher when your subconscious is working with you, not against you.

In chapter 3 we look at exactly how you can optimise brain function for advanced mental clarity, focus and concentration. You may be surprised how this is done.

Chapter 3

How to Optimise Brain Function for Mental Clarity, Heightened Focus and Concentration

FOR MANY YEARS it was believed that the brain was hard-wired and fixed and that its growth was fully established by the time we reach adulthood. With advances in functional brain imaging technology we now know this is not true and our brains can continually learn, change, and express more potential throughout our entire lives. The brain's adaptability and capacity for change is called 'neuroplasticity'.

The major brain cells that allow the brain to be an information processor are called neurons, and we have about one hundred billion of them. Neurons form information networks called neuronets that communicate the information from the brain to the body and vice-versa. As we integrate new beliefs and behaviours we form new neuronets which we strengthen and develop by taking action toward our goals, giving us more choices and enhancing and expanding our abilities.

How Powerful are You?
To get an idea of how powerful your brain is, imagine every single person on earth, all 7 billion-ish of us, with a hand calculator performing a calculation every five seconds for sixty hours. Okay, got your head around that? The world's most powerful computers, called supercomputers, can perform the same amount of calculations in just one second.

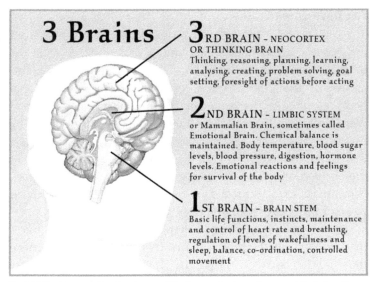

3 Brains

3RD BRAIN - NEOCORTEX OR THINKING BRAIN
Thinking, reasoning, planning, learning, analysing, creating, problem solving, goal setting, foresight of actions before acting

2ND BRAIN - LIMBIC SYSTEM or Mammalian Brain, sometimes called Emotional Brain. Chemical balance is maintained. Body temperature, blood sugar levels, blood pressure, digestion, hormone levels. Emotional reactions and feelings for survival of the body

1ST BRAIN - BRAIN STEM
Basic life functions, instincts, maintenance and control of heart rate and breathing, regulation of levels of wakefulness and sleep, balance, co-ordination, controlled movement

Fig 3.0:The three major structures of the human brain and some of their functions.

That's an accomplishment that blows our minds, until we realise that it would take three of these supercomputers linked together to map the connections to just one single neuronet firing in the human brain! And a piece of brain the size of a grain of salt contains approximately one hundred thousand neurons with a billion connections to other neurons. That is a lot of processing power! The total number of permutations and combinations of brain connections, and hence potential, is almost infinite. As leading brain researcher at the University of Pennsylvania, Dr Andrew Newburg says,

> *"We have astonishing potential to change the autopilot behaviours and patterns we have fallen into. Using the right tools and intentions, the potential for change within our nervous system, within our entire physiology is tremendous."*

You Have Three Brains

The brain is basically a three-fold structure that grows from the bottom up as it develops (see **Fig 3.0**). First there is the brainstem or hind brain; then the mid brain, which is also known as the limbic system or mammalian or emotional brain (containing the amygdala and hippocampus); and then there is the neocortex or forebrain (the 'thinking brain'). The neocortex is split into two halves, a left and right hemisphere. Research pioneered by Paul Maclean, M.D., suggests that the three brains amount to three interconnected biological computers. Each possesses its own intelligence, subjectivity, sense of time and space, memory and other functions.

The amygdala is an almond-shaped group of neurons that is situated deep in the limbic brain. Its primary role is alerting the body in survival situations. It also helps to correlate different emotional charges to your long-term memories. If anything in your environment reminds your subconscious memory banks of a past experience that was threatening or felt uncomfortable, your amygdala will activate, sending your body into the survival response of fight or flight. Back when we were primitive beings exposed to the dangers of the environment, it was appropriate for us to respond to these flight-or-fight signals. If a tiger was coming at you, you would want to flee back to your cave to safety. But in today's modern world, you are not subject to many such life-or-death threats. Your amygdala, however, still responds to perceived threats, which more often than not are psychological rather than physical. Your emotions are constantly provoked – from anger to frustration to embarrassment and guilt – as you negotiate the complexities of your busy days and complex relationships. Today, we call this response 'stress'. The constant pressure of stress on your system is as real as the sudden flow of chemicals that sent your primitive ancestors fleeing from tigers, and stress can wear you down, effecting your health and state of well-being. When under stress, your critical thinking and decision-making are diminished, and you are more likely to act irrationally.

We have a big brain that is for learning, creating, remembering and speculating possibilities, but when it is driven by the emotional brain, all of the awareness that could be used for new possibilities is now being endorsed and governed by a primitive survival system.

As you increase your conscious awareness and clear your memory banks' of out-dated beliefs and perceptions, your body can react better to changes in the environment, you become more resilient to change and your mental clarity and emotional balance increases.

The cortex is the king of your brain. It is very large in humans, compared to the rest of the animal world, which explains our higher thinking capacities, especially self-awareness.

The frontal lobes are the most highly evolved area of the human brain. Your frontal lobes enable you to direct your attention, initiate behaviours, reason and rationalise. The greater the frontal lobe activity the less propensity we have for impulsive activity and emotional behaviour.

Your brain's cortex, as I said, is split into two halves: a left and right hemisphere. Each hemisphere has its own unique overall functions, which allow you to perceive the world in different ways. (See Fig 3.1) Generally speaking, the left hemisphere is the seat of intellect in the guise of logic and reasoning, especially as the seat of ideas that are communicated through language. The right hemisphere is the seat of creativity and holistic thinking.

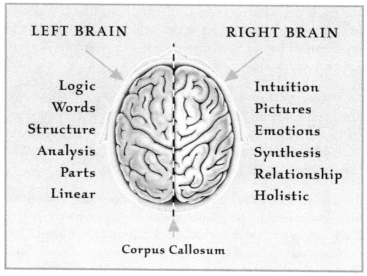

LEFT BRAIN   **RIGHT BRAIN**

LEFT BRAIN	RIGHT BRAIN
Logic	Intuition
Words	Pictures
Structure	Emotions
Analysis	Synthesis
Parts	Relationship
Linear	Holistic

Corpus Callosum

Fig 3.1: The two hemispheres of your cortex have their own unique functions, bestowing different gifts. Generally speaking, the left hemisphere is the seat of logic and reasoning, whereas the right hemisphere is the seat of intuition and creativity.

It encodes for spatial reasoning and links you to the world through the medium of your feelings. Throughout your life, you will tend to develop dominance in one hemisphere over the other, which can limit you in how much of your potential and wisdom you can access in each moment. As a sweeping generalisation, if you grew up in a household where your creative and artistic talents were emphasised and where you were supported in trusting your feelings, imagination and intuition, your right hemisphere may be well developed and your left not so. Alternatively, if you grew up in a household where logic, structure and linear processes were the main ways of perceiving the world, your left hemisphere may have dominance in your life. Interestingly, the hemispheric connections do not become fully mature until about the age of ten. When both sides of your brain are developed equally and so working together harmoniously, you have a very different view of the world than if one hemisphere is dominant.

As another generalisation, the western world has a heavy bias in the left hemispheric way of functioning, relying as it does on facts and science, logic and reasoning. Often the corporate mind-set is so fixed on systems and processes that there is little room for employees to express their creative, innovative and intuitive abilities. Management is fixated on their employees 'doing things the right way' (which usually means the way things have always been done), and so they tend to value fidelity to the status quo over the risk-taking behaviours of change and innovation. Our educational systems are also heavily biased toward developing our left hemispheric talents, focusing as they do on consensual knowledge, facts, rote learning, science and mathematics, and less on creative expression, artistic exploration, and out-of-the-box thinking.

Phase Lock Your Brain to Maximise Performance

The two hemispheres of the brain are connected by a band of fibres called the corpus callosum. This bridge allows information to be shared between both hemispheres creating more brain potential.

> For peak performance you need maximum activity in the frontal lobes and integrated left and right hemispheres to create a 'whole brain state'.

As Professor at Youngstown Christopher M. Bache in his book Dark Night, Early Dawn tells us,

> "When the brain's hemispheres are phase-locked and work as one, a number of known benefits result, including heightened awareness, improved recall, enhanced self-programming flexibility, and increased creativity—in short, you increase your capacity for super learning."

You will learn how to do this in Chapter 4 with the Gamma Brain Technique.

The Power of Your Heart and Peak Performance

Most of us think of the heart as a pump that propels blood around the body. That's certainly what I was taught in physiology classes at college. This is true, of course; but researchers at the leading edge of science are telling us it is so much more than a mere pump. The trouble is, this information is not widely known.

Scientific evidence has shown that the heart has over forty thousand brain cells of its own and sends emotional and intuitive information signals to the brain and body. The heart is our main electrical power centre. It produces two and a half watts of electrical power, which is 40 to 60 times more wattage than is produced by the electrical activity of the brain. Interestingly, you can record your heart beat anywhere on your body. That is because every time your heart beats, the electrical field it produces permeates every cell, forming a body-wide communication network. Your thoughts and feelings are communicated to every cell of your body with every heartbeat! What is more, this electromagnetic field doesn't just radiate throughout your body, but actually streams from you to the outside world, in a 360-degree field that is shaped like a torus (a ring doughnut) and that radiates up to 15 feet outside your body. It is actually thought to extend much further, but our current measuring equipment can only confirm its extension to this distance. (**See Fig 3.2**)

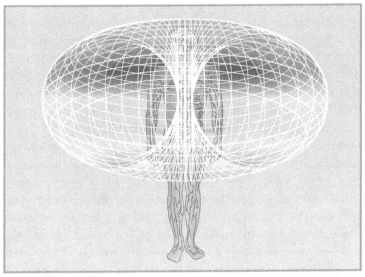

Fig 3.2: An actual image of the heart field radiating from the body. Changes in our emotional states change the information field we broadcast. Very literally we are broadcasting how we feel 24 hours a day!

You Broadcast Your Emotions 24 Hours a Day

That our heart field extends so far outside our body may explain why we can sense 'emotional atmospheres' so easily. The frequencies of the heart actually change depending on how we feel. Our emotional state influences changes in our electromagnetic information signature which we more commonly call our 'personal vibration' or 'vibe'. Since its field is much more powerful than the brain's, it stands to reason that it is a more powerful 'detector' than the brain. This may be why you immediately sense 'something wrong' when you walk into a room, or, conversely, may immediately feel a space is 'sacred' or 'special'. We are all literally broadcasting our emotional state into our environment all the time!

How Your Emotional State Unlocks Your Brain's Potential

Your perceptions of your environment are communicated to your heart by part of your brain and body's communication system called the autonomic nervous system. The autonomic nervous system has two branches, the parasympathetic and the sympathetic. The sympathetic controls the bodily processes that have to do with energy utilisation, sometimes known as fight and flight. The other branch, the parasympathetic system, controls bodily activities having to do with energy conservation, sometimes called the rest and digest system. The sympathetic is the accelerator and the parasympathetic is the brake of your body. Stress causes an imbalance in these two systems and harmonising the two is a key to increased physical, mental and emotional energy and peak performance.

When you feel angry, frustrated or stressed, your heart rhythms reflect the state of your being. In this case, they would move away from a smooth, coherent pattern, becoming more erratic and random, like looking at a graph of an earthquake (see Fig 3.3). This incoherent pattern causes a release of stress hormones, such as adrenaline and cortisol, which dampen the activity of the higher centres of your brain, including your frontal lobes - responsible for conscious thinking and what we think of as the 'wisdom' centre since it is active in decision making. You may have noticed in the past that when you fly into anger, your ability to solve problems or make wise decisions is diminished. That's because when you perceive a situation as stressful, your body shunts blood to where it is most needed, which is to the lower, more primitive areas of your brain that put you into a flight-or-fight response. In

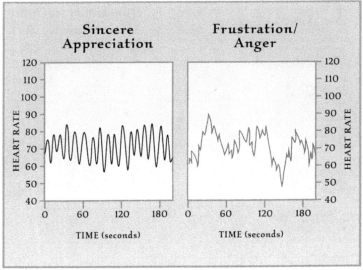

Fig 3.3: Two heart-beat patterns: the one on the left is the heart rhythm of someone who is feeling appreciation, the one on the right, of someone who is experiencing anger. The coherent pattern on the left is the state that is conducive to health and learning, so it is the state of being most conducive to letting go of old, self-sabotaging beliefs and reprogramming the brain.

contrast, when you feel happiness, appreciation, kindness or just simply feel relaxed, your heart goes into a rhythm that is highly ordered and coherent and your brain's cortex experiences heightened activity, allowing for more awareness and expression of your potential (**see Fig 3.4**).

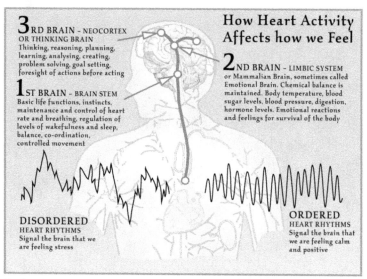

Fig 3.4: The two hemispheres of your cortex have their own unique functions, bestowing different gifts. Generally speaking, the left hemisphere is the seat of logic and reasoning, whereas the right hemisphere is the seat of intuition and creativity.

Your heart rhythm is said to be 'coherent' when both branches of your autonomic nervous system are working in unison, which is known as 'entrainment'. When your brain, heart, thoughts and feelings are all in balance, you move into a super focused mind and peak performance state. This is achieved when you use the Gamma Brain Technique which you will learn next.

Chapter 4

Program Your Subconscious Mind for Success - The Gamma Brain Technique©

MOST PEOPLE HAVE BEEN CONDITIONED to think of change as difficult and threatening rather than exciting, liberating and self-affirming. It's a truism that, as the old saying goes, 'The only people who like change are cashiers and wet babies.' But that is the out-dated view about change. Now that you know about the mind-body connection and the heart-brain connection – you can powerfully program your mind and body to create new levels of success.

Over forty years ago a form of psychology known as 'Energy Psychology' was developed. It is based on both the eastern and western understanding of the energy systems of the body and the latest principles of how your mind communicates information– beliefs, thoughts and feelings, as I have laid out for you in the previous chapters. The Gamma Brain Technique and Emotional Balance Technique (see Part 2 Managing Your Emotions) are leading edge energy psychology techniques. You will now be working at this cutting edge level to repattern your brain, update your mind and achieve peak functioning. There are four main ways to use this technique:

1. To program your subconscious mind with new empowering beliefs and goals.

Fig 4.0: Sit ankles crossed (it doesn't matter which foot is on top)

Fig 4.1: Cross one wrist over the other (it doesn't matter which arm is on top).

Fig 4.2: Bring your clasped palms up to your middle chest/heart area

Fig 4.3: The full Whole Brain posture

2. To achieve a heightened state of awareness and focus for meetings, presentations etc.

3. To solve problems.

4. As a rest and renewal meditation.

1. Using the Gamma Brain Technique to Program your Subconscious Mind.

1. Sit in the 'whole brain posture' and close your eyes. (**See Figs 4.0 - 4.3**). Take 3 deep belly breaths and relax all your muscles, especially the face and jaw, let the whole body relax. Spend 30 seconds or so focusing on relaxing your face and body.

2. Think of a situation that evokes strong feelings of appreciation, happiness, gratitude, love, or other positive heart based emotions. Maybe memories of holding your baby son or daughter, a day of your favourite holiday, your favourite scenery, someone you love, a special moment in your life, or the like. Really connect in with the emotional aspects of the experience and really amplify these feelings throughout your whole body.

3. Silently and slowly repeat the belief statement as if you are sending it into every part of your body. Continue silently repeating the belief statement silently until you feel some sort of internal signal that your brain and body has integrated this new information. This 'signal' can take any number of forms or feelings, such as a feeling that energy is moving within your body, visual impressions, feelings, memories, very often a deeper sense of relaxation and changes in your breathing, body movements or twitches. It's okay not to feel anything different as well – just wait until you feel intuitively that the information is integrated. Generally, the signal will be quick, often within a minute or two of assuming the posture. Saturate yourself with these positive feelings as you repeat the belief statement silently. When you feel complete, open your eyes, take a deep belly breath and come out of the whole brain posture.

In appendix A you will find over 180 belief statements to integrate into your brain and body if you feel they will enhance your life and improve your performance. Alternatively you can simply create your own specific belief statements relevant to your goals.

Creating Your Own Belief Statements

Creating and integrating your own belief statements is an essential part of programming your mind for success. Here are the guidelines for creating them:

- The more specific you are in the wording of your belief statements, the more effective they are.
- Use the first person tense. Make 'I' statements.
- Start your belief statements with phrases such as; I do, I am, I deserve, I can, It is easy for me to and so on.
- Word your statements in the positive; for example, instead of writing 'I am not anxious of speaking in front of my peers', reword your belief statement as 'I communicate with confidence and clarity in front of my peers'.
- Make your belief statements meaningful to you, when you say it to yourself the statement really resonates and makes you feel like that's something you want.
- The belief statements in Appendix A will give you some good ideas.

■ ■ ■

1.How Many Times do You Need to Use the Technique before a Belief is integrated Into the brain and Body?

Let's say you are integrating a belief about your presentation abilities and you are using; *'I communicate my skills, knowledge and experience in presentations with confidence and clarity'*. You would simply do this every day until you feel that you are confident in achieving the goal. This may just need a one off-one minute integration or need to be repeated over several days. In this example using the Emotional Balance Technique that you will learn in the *Managing your Emotions* section to remove the fear and anxiety would also enhance the speed of the integration.

2. Using the Gamma Brain Technique to Achieve a Heightened State of Awareness and Focus.

You can use this technique to prepare yourself for a meeting, presentation, important/difficult conversation, to be calm, centred and present or anytime you need to de-stress and move into balance and a super focused mind state. Do steps 1 and 2 of the above procedure and when you feel relaxed, balanced and calm slowly come out of the technique and move into your next task with increased awareness. You can also add specific visualisations of your desired outcomes into the process.

3. The Gamma Brain Technique and Problem Solving.

When you have a problem and you need some creative solution focused ideas, do the following; a) Be very clear on your problem and intend to get some clarity on a solution and the best way to proceed. b) Perform steps 1 and 2 of the technique. c) When you are deeply relaxed and your mind is calm, ask, "How can I solve this situation?" What do I need to do for the best outcome for all?" and other relevant questions. Remain relaxed and just experience what pops into your mind.

Remember you are putting your brain into a peak functioning state. I suggest having a notepad and pen close by when you do this as often your brain will 'serve up' ideas and answers whilst in this deep state of relaxation. Answers and ideas also pop into your mind after completion of the technique when you are thinking about something else entirely.

4. The Gamma Brain Technique Rest and Renewal Meditation.
You also want to use this technique as a rest and renewal meditation at least once a day. Perform steps 1 and 2 and move into that relaxed, calm state. With each breath relax even more. The only goal is to relax. Just 5-10 minutes of this meditation creates a profound sense of physical, mental and emotional relaxation and rejuvenation.

Why The Gamma Brain Technique Works.
- What Exactly Happens in the Brain when Using The Gamma Brain Technique? In February 2011 at the 'Learning with Neuro-Feedback Centre' in London I measured participant's brain activity as they used The Gamma Brain Technique. The results were outstanding. Within as little as 40 seconds of deep immersion in this technique there is an increase in alpha and theta brain-waves showing a relaxed body and an increase in coherency between left and right hemispheres. There is also a huge level of gamma brain wave activity in the frontal lobes of the brain. As a reminder, gamma waves create a super focused mind state and the more activity you create in the frontal lobes the more potential you can express. This is the premium state you want to train your brain to access. The more you use this technique the more naturally your brain will access high performance states. **Learn the Gamma Brain Technique in the free video training at www.ChrisWaltonUK.com.**

- The 'whole brain posture' was devised by Dr Paul Dennison. It is an effective and simple way to use your body to help facilitate the alignment of the left and right hemispheres of your brain, so that they better communicate with one another. The right hemisphere controls the left motor functions of the body and vice-versa, by crossing your arms and legs at the midline of your body, you ensure that you are activating both hemispheres and creating what's termed a 'whole-brain' state. With the eyes closed, this posture very quickly creates a high level of alpha brain wave activity. This relaxes the body and leads to heightened levels of intuition, creativity, focus and an optimal balance between intelligence and logic and wisdom and insight.

- The heart is the powerhouse of the process. Remember from chapter 3 that your heart and brain are constantly sending signals to each other and that feelings of gratitude, happiness, appreciation etc., directly activate your brains frontal lobes, the most evolved part of your brain. The frontal lobes quieten down the areas of the brain to do with bodily sensations and the emotional centres. In this peak brain state, silently repeating the belief statement creates electrical activity in the brain, influencing the body's chemical output and sending the information throughout the entire body. The new belief is mapped and patterned as a set of 'electro-chemical' connections which allow you to create new ways of thinking, new behaviours, and express new levels of potential.

Integrating a new belief program into the brain is rather like downloading a new piece of software into your computer. In a computer, there are a specific set of pathways dedicated to routing the information to the proper place in the hard drive's memory chips. Once the information is loaded, you can easily access it by simply clicking an icon. In your mind and body a similar process occurs. Your new belief is loaded into your subconscious mind, held there once it is fully integrated, and then is ready for you to access in your daily life – opening the way for new, inspired and self-empowering actions and behaviours. You can create new brain patterns for every area of your life.

MAXIMISE YOUR ENERGY, RESILIENCE AND PERFORMANCE ACTION STEP 2:

- Every day use the Gamma Brain Technique to integrate new empowering beliefs into your subconscious mind.
- Use the technique at key times throughout the day to achieve a super focused mind state or solve problems.
- Use the technique as a 5-10 minute rest and renewal meditation at least once a day, ideally mid-afternoon when your body most craves rest. (You will learn more about this in the Managing Your Body section.)

OK so now you've learned how to create a super focused mind and reprogram your subconscious beliefs. In Part 2, Managing Your Emotions, you will learn why having a high level of emotional intelligence is an absolute necessity to maximise your energy, resilience and performance. Firstly let's understand the impact emotions have on our health and energy and learn the Emotional Balance Technique to eliminate psychological and emotional stress.

■ ■ ■

Part 2

Managing Your Emotions

Chapter 5

Using Your Emotions to Maximise Your Energy, Resilience and Performance

When dealing with people, remember you are not dealing with creatures of logic but creatures of emotion.
Dale Carnegie

WHAT ARE EMOTIONS? Emotion is "energy in motion". The word itself is derived from the Latin verb meaning "to move". Emotional energy adds power to your thoughts. Scientists used to think that emotions are produced only in the brain. However, sophisticated instruments now show that emotions are the product of an on-going dialogue between the body and the brain. Our emotional experience normally on a scale from very pleasant to very painful is really a combination of feeling sensations, associated mental thoughts and biochemical reactions.

As we saw in the Managing Your Mind section, every time we think a thought we instantly have an emotional feeling to match that thought. It is these thoughts and feelings that create specific chemicals that are absorbed into our cells that give rise to how we feel. If we have self-depreciating or stressful thoughts we instantly start to feel negative, unhappy or unworthy. If we have focused, confident thoughts we instantly start to feel optimistic, positive and so on. Thoughts and feelings are intimately connected which is a blessing and a curse.

When we start to think negatively we create the chemicals that make us feel negative. When feeling negative we start to think more negatively and we can get caught in a vicious cycle of think-feel-think-feel-think-feel all day long. And most of this is done on 'autopilot' with little if any awareness. Now here's the rub:

If we cannot think greater than we feel we can never change! Our whole personality, our whole identity, our whole being becomes conditioned into certain parameters of success due to our mostly unconscious pre-programmed thoughts and feelings. This is why a high level of emotional awareness and management is essential to maximise your performance and success.

Most people ride the same autopilot rollercoaster of thoughts and emotions day in and day out. On average we experience almost 30 different emotional states each hour. With about 16-17 waking hours each day that's over 450 emotions every day and over 3000 emotional reactions each week. As the majority of these emotional reactions are occurring whilst we are at work, it is quite obvious that people with high levels of emotional intelligence are easier to work with and higher performers.

The Emotions of Peak Performance

EXERCISE:
1. What are the 3 key emotions that you feel when you are performing at your best?
2. Take a look at the diagram below (**Fig 5.0**) and just consider how many of these emotions you experience on a regular basis. How often do you feel the emotions in the left hand column? And how often do you consciously choose them or are they autopilot reactions?

UNRESOURCEFUL STATE	RESOURCEFUL STATE
Anger	Happy
Frustration	Joyous
Sadness	Resiliant
Lethargy	Free
Jealousy	Energised
Hate	Purposeful
Stressed	Content
Envy	Motivated
Worried	Balanced
Anxious	Love
Bitter	Compassion
Resentful	Empathy
Greed	Awareness
Guilt	Exhilarated
Rejection	Excited
Insecurity	Determined
Uncertainty	Elated
	Calm

Fig 5.0: Emotional States

Few of us will consciously choose to be in the left hand column. We access these emotions unconsciously, reactively and instinctively. In order to effectively utilise the amazing power of emotion we need to become very conscious of which emotions add quality to our lives and which ones do not.

The evidence is very clear; negative emotions keep your brain and body bathed in stress hormones. This speeds up your 'biological aging clock', draining emotional buoyancy and physical vitality. In fact, researchers have found that emotional stress is one of the strongest risk factors for heart disease and sudden cardiac arrest, as much as, or more so than smoking or a sedentary life style. One hormone to pay close attention to is adrenaline. Strong emotions, like anger or fear, release a lot of adrenaline into your body. Adrenaline gives you a boost, like a cup of coffee, it can make you hyper aware for a short period of time. This can be useful in some situations, but too much adrenaline can lead to high blood pressure and burnout. I have coached many 'stressed-out' city clients who have thrived on the adrenaline buzz mistakenly thinking it is a high performance zone and ended up with long term fatigue. Another hormone that gets released when we are feeling stressful emotions is cortisol. Studies by Dr Bruce McEwen, the director of the neuroendocrinology lab at Rockefeller University in New York, found that the stress hormone cortisol wears down the brain, leading to atrophy and memory loss. It also raises blood pressure and blood sugar, which contributes to hardening arteries, which in turn may lead to heart disease. Managing our emotional stress is essential if we want to increase our energy and resilience.

The Health Effects of Stress

The effects of stress in people are seen physically, mentally and emotionally. According to the American Institute of Stress, up to 90% of all health problems are related to stress. Too much stress can contribute to and agitate many health problems including heart disease, high blood pressure, stroke, depression and sleep disorders. Three 10-year studies concluded that emotional stress was more predictive of death from cancer and cardiovascular disease than smoking. *People who were ineffectively managing stress had a 40% higher death rate than non-stressed individuals!*

- In a 2007 study, the number of workers who had sought medical advice for what they believed to be work related stress increased by 110,000 to an estimated 530,000.
- Even mild stress has been proven to lead to people being unable to work. The research carried out by the University of Bristol and the Karolinska Institute in Sweden revealed that mild stress increases the chance of someone being on disability payments for physical problems by 70 per cent and more than doubles the likelihood they will have a psychiatric condition.

The Most Effective Way to Eliminate Psychological and Emotional Stress

The Emotional Balance Technique uses specific acupuncture points to eliminate psychological and emotional stress. To satisfy our logical left brain, first some understanding of how and why this works.

Most people have heard of acupuncture, not surprisingly since it has been around for 5000 years. However it wasn't until recently that western science validated this as a 'real sys-tem'. Acupuncture uses meridians which are vessels or channels of energy that circulate throughout the body just under the skin carrying and regulating vital energy. They are accessed through acupuncture points on the skin. The western medical establishment finally caught up with the Chinese in 1995, as the existence of energy channels running in the body exactly where the Chinese plotted them was confirmed by experiment. Dr Pierre de Vernejoul and his team injected a non-toxic radioactive tracer dye into the legs of his volunteers at the commonly used acupuncture points of the meridian system. He then used gamma camera imaging to trace the flow of the dye. His team found that the radioactive dye travelled specifically along the clearly defined meridian network that the Chinese have been using for thousands of years. When the dye was injected elsewhere in the body, randomly and not at known acupuncture points, it did not move along any specific pathway. This work began a period of more intensive study by other researchers of the meridian system, which Chinese medical doctor Ted Kaptchuk described as:

"An invisible network that links together all the relevant substances and organs of the body"

In another scientific validation of the acupuncture meridians, professor of physics Zang-Hee Cho, from the University of California, Irvine, discovered that pressure on the vision-related acupuncture points on the outside of the foot almost instantaneously activates the visual cortex in the brain, as measured by a functional brain scan. See **Fig 5.1**. In fact, acupuncture needling these specific points on the foot had the same impact on the brain as shining a torch light into the participant's eyes! Many studies have shown that the meridian pathways are low resistance pathways for the flow of electricity. As Dr James Oschman concludes, *"The meridians then are simply the main channels or transmission lines in the continuous molecular fabric of the body."*

Research at Harvard Medical School by Dr Bruce Rosen showed that needling an acupuncture point on the hand known as Large Intestine 4, which is believed to help ease pain, caused immediate blood flow changes to the amygdala and related areas of the brain that correlate with pain, mood, emotions and cravings. The reduction in blood flow to these areas lead to an increase in endorphins, the brains natural pain relieving pleasure chemicals. Other research showed that activating specific acupuncture points correlated with enhanced serotonin secretion. Serotonin is our feel-good chemical.

This research and other studies have shown without a doubt that activating particular acupuncture points correlates to specific effects in precise areas of the brain.

■ ■ ■

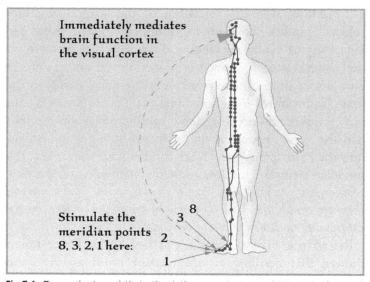

Fig 5.1: Research showed that stimulating acupuncture points on the foot that were said by the Chinese to stimulate the eyes and vision did indeed stimulate the visual cortex, even though there is no known mechanism in traditional medicine or biology to explain this cause-effect phenomenon.

Even applying pressure to acupuncture points, called acupressure, instead of inserting needles, produces very effective results. The benefits of such non-invasive techniques can be enormous. For example, acupuncture and acupressure can calm deep brain structures, such as the limbic system. When the limbic system is activated, your nervous system initiates a body-wide fight-or-flight response, which induces stress and causes your prefrontal cortex, your higher thought centre, to go 'offline' temporarily. Knowing some acupressure points can help you easily reduce the impact of negative and persistent emotional patterns, memories and reactions that may have been causing stress on your nervous system for years, limiting your potential.

You do not need to be an acupuncturist to benefit from using your meridian system to enhance your health and well-being. Applying pressure with your fingers to the proper points is all that it takes to produce excellent results. Psychological issues, fears, anxieties and other stressors create a disturbance in the body's electrical systems and some of the meridians can 'seize up' like a kink in a garden hose. Tapping the acupuncture points stimulates the receptors on your skin. These touch receptors respond by transferring signals to the respective nerve centres of the brain. If you recall an emotional problem and begin tapping the appropriate acupuncture point, signals are sent to your brain, and the pathways associated with this emotional problem are disrupted, the neurochemical endorphins (endorphins are 27 times more powerful than morphine) are released and the emotional energy is diffused and reimprinted so that the pathways will not be activated in the same way again. This is an easy and effective way to recondition your subconscious and improve your capacity for positive change. Out of many techniques you can use to work with emotions this is by far the most powerful and effective for clearing emotional stress.

The Emotional Balance Technique©
(Learn this in a free video training course at
www.ChrisWaltonUK.com)

- Think of an issue, person, event or situation that causes you stress. It should be something that provokes an emotional charge, a reaction and feeling that you would rather not have. Something that holds you back from performing at your best. Perhaps doing a presentation to peers or a meeting with your boss or discussing a project that is running over its completion date etc.

- Rate the level of stress you get from the issue on a scale of one to ten, with ten being a highly charged feeling and one being not really an issue.
- To disconnect the emotional charge from an issue tap the ten meridian points shown in Fig 5.2 according to the directions in the numbered list below. I will describe the method before listing the tapping point order.

1. Continue to think of and feel the effects of the issue as you tap the points. Use short statements about the issue such as 'angry with my boss' which you would repeat through the entire sequence of tapping.

2. The tapping pressure is firm but not hard.

3. Tap the points six times each in the following order, tap using all four fingers and thumb.

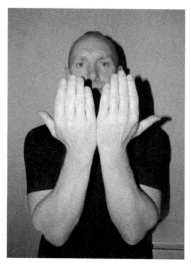

Fig 5.2

Fig 5.2.1: Sides of the hands together
(Small intestine meridian; removes self-doubt, feelings of low self-esteem and improves self-confidencecause-effect phenomenon.

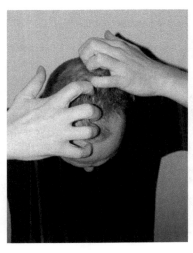

Fig 5.2.2: Crown suture, a straight line from the crown of your head to your forehead.
(You do not need to bend your head down, that is for demonstration purposes only. Many meridians meet at the top of the head, removes self-critical thinking and lack of focus)

Fig 5.2.3: Eyebrows
(Bladder meridian; removes trauma, hurt, sadness, frustration, impatience, improves inner peace and calm)

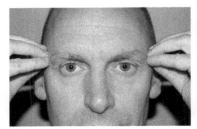

Fig 5.2.4: Temples
(Gall bladder meridian; removes rage, anger, resentment, fear of change, improves clarity and compassion)

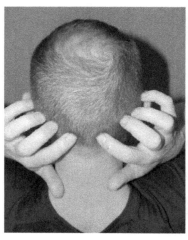

Fig 5.2.5: Back of the head, where the top of the neck joins the skull.
Several meridians run over the head, this point helps remove all of the above emotions.

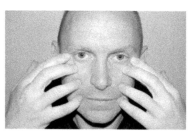

Fig 5.2.6: Side of lips to side of eyes - index finger on edge of eye, little finger to corner of mouth
(Stomach and small intestine meridian; removes fear, anxiety, emptiness, worry, nervousness, loneliness and disappointment, helps improve calmness, contentment and feeling safe)

Fig 5.2.7: Under nose
(Governing meridian; removes embarassment, powerlessness, shame guilt, grief, fear of ridicule, helps improve self-acceptance, personal power and compassion for self and others)

Fig 5.2.8: Under bottom lip
(Central meridian removes: confusion, uncertainty, shame, embarrassment, helps improve clarity, certainty and confidence)

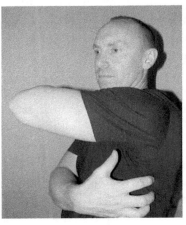

Fig 5.2.9: Four inches under the armpits - Tap both sides
(Spleen meridian removes: guilt, worry, obsessing, hopelessness, insecurity, helps improve clarity, confidence and relaxation)

Fig 5.2.10: Your collarbone/thymus point approximately 2 inches down from your sternal notch
(Kidney meridian removes: indecision, feeling stuck, worry, fear, helps improve confidence and clarity to move forward)

When you have finished the tapping procedure, check in emotionally and rate your stress about the issue again, using the same scale of one to ten. The intensity of the emotion should have dropped at least 2 points and sometimes cleared completely. Repeat the technique until the issue doesn't bother you anymore.

People who use this meridian tapping technique report dramatically reduced stress and 'emotional charge' around the issue allowing them to move forward and make conscious decisions with clarity and wisdom. There may be several aspects to an issue, for example one of my coaching clients was angry about how she was being treated by her boss. We removed the anger, then she began to feel frustration that she was not treated fairly, she then moved to feeling anxious and then demotivated and lethargic about her work in general. After about five rounds of tapping the ten acupoints she was free of these emotional reactions and could not get them back! You keep going until you have worked through all the issues that you feel are draining your emotional energy and throwing your system off balance. This is very powerful and takes just minutes. Using this simple but effective technique is a safe and free way to maintain or increase your emotional and mental health and improve your resilience. On a physical level, you are removing stress from your nervous system, which is freeing up energy for you to do more. On an emotional level, this new reservoir of energy can help you better express who you are and so help you better utilise your gifts and talents. These ten acupuncture points can treat issues such as embarrassment, trauma, anxiety, anger, impatience, frustration and even depression. They rapidly enhance immune system function and these ten points power up the entire meridian system increasing health and energy throughout your whole mind and body.

When to use this Technique

You can use this technique at any time to boost your energy circuits. It is good to do in the shower in the morning to make sure your energy is flowing optimally. If you have some anxiety about a meeting, a difficult conversation or some area of the day you feel stressed about, it is an excellent idea to use this beforehand. Also at the end of the day to clear the stressors of the day from your body leaving you more balanced when you walk in your front door to your personal life.

MAXIMISE YOUR ENERGY, RESILIENCE AND PERFORMANCE ACTION STEP 3:
Clear your emotional stressors one at a time. Use the Emotional Balance Technique as often as required until you feel emotionally clear and balanced and you are reacting less and less from your autopilot emotional brain.

Obviously it is better for us to experience emotions that allow us to perform at our best and improve our health and wellbeing and hence why Emotional Intelligence is such a key element to maximising performance. So are you emotionally intelligent? Let's find out...

Chapter 6

Using Emotional Intelligence to Maximise Your Energy, Resilience and Performance

R ESEARCH SHOW US that emotional intelligence (E.I.) is the single biggest predictor of performance in the workplace and the strongest driver of leadership and personal excellence. Emotional Intelligence is most easily described in **Fig 6.0** below.

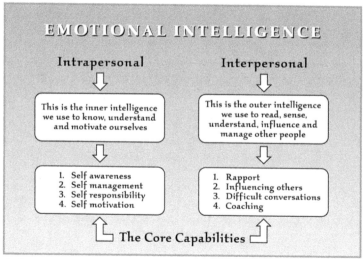

Fig 6.0: The Key Aspects of Emotional Intelligence

It is very clear that developing emotional intelligence does improve performance. We make all our decisions at an emotional level (because our emotional brain developed before our thinking brain.) and then justify our decisions logically with our thinking brain. Becoming more emotionally conscious has a huge impact on your decision making and inevitably your success.

What would it be like if your Workplace was Emotionally Intelligent?

Studies by emotional intelligence researchers Dr Travis Bradbury and Dr Jean Greaves have shown that 90% of high performers score very high in E.I. profiles as opposed to just 20% of low performers have a high level of E.I. Research at the University of Queensland in Australia showed that employees that scored low in job performance and emotional intelligence could match their high performance – highly emotionally intelligent colleagues solely by working on their emotional intelligence. A study carried out by The Carnegie Institute of Technology into why people are successful in business concluded that 85% of financial success is due to skills in human engineering and only 15% is due to technical knowledge. Human engineering comes from two of the fundamental aspects of emotional intelligence; self-management and relationship management. When we understand how are brains work we can see that measuring, understanding and developing our emotional intelligence is an essential factor to performing at our best especially when change is so rapid and volatile. Imagine what it would be like if your workplace was full of people that:

- Took full responsibility for their emotional reactions.

- Was a culture where people take unconditional responsibility for their actions and results

- Knew how to monitor and channel their emotional energy and stress levels.
- Had high levels of self-esteem, confidence and behavioural flexibility.
- Were highly self-motivated.
- Understood how to connect and build deep rapport and trust with others.
- Handled conflict with wisdom and integrity.
- Had a flexible and agile mentality creating innovative ideas.

If all external market forces are equal, a highly emotionally intelligent organisation will be a highly successful organisation and a happier environment to work in.

Measuring your Emotional Intelligence

Below are 16 key aspects of Emotional Intelligence. Reflect on each question and give yourself an honest self-appraisal of how emotionally intelligent you are.

1. **SELF-REGARD (Self-Esteem).**

   How much do you value yourself as a person? Liking and accepting yourself and having a high level of self-esteem is obviously the bedrock for any type of high performance.

2. **REGARD FOR OTHERS.**

   How much do you value others? How often do you see people as 'objects' rather than people with hopes, fears, insecurities and goals like all human beings? How often do you judge others based on your beliefs and rules?

3. **SELF-AWARENESS.**

    How aware are you of what you are thinking, feeling and doing at any given moment? How conscious are you? How aware are you of the messages your body is giving you? Your gut feel, your intuitions - thousands of times a day your emotional brain sends signals to you via feelings and bodily sensations. People with low awareness often miss these or ignore them.

4. **AWARENESS OF OTHERS.**

    How good are you at understanding how other people are feeling? How good are you at picking up all the non-verbal communication from people?

5. **EMOTIONAL RESILIENCE.**

    How effectively do you recover from emotional setbacks? How good are you at turning overwhelming and negative feelings into productivity, emotional stability and balance?

6. **PERSONAL POWER.**

    How much do you take responsibility for your own life and take responsibility for your actions and results?

7. **GOAL DIRECTEDNESS.**

    How clear are you on your goals and how well are your beliefs and emotions in alignment with these goals? How productive are your action steps toward these goals or are you a chief procrastinator?

8. **FLEXIBILITY.**

    How good are you at adapting your thoughts, feelings, attitudes, behaviours and actions in the rapidly changing world we live in? How much do you resist change?

9. **PERSONAL CONNECTEDNESS.**

   How honest are you with yourself about how you feel? How do you feel communicating this to others?

10. **INVITATION TO TRUST.**

    How much do you invite the trust of others by being reliable and true to your word? How often do you say things you do not really mean? How often do you change your opinion just to be liked by those around you?

11. **TRUST.**

    Do you have a balanced outlook on trust? Do you trust others too much, not enough? Are you overly sceptical?

12. **BALANCED OUTLOOK.**

    What's your balance between optimism and pessimism?

13. **EMOTIONAL EXPRESSION AND CONTROL.**

    As the hundreds of emotions flow through every day, do you bottle them up? Do you express them healthily? Can you express your emotions in appropriate ways at appropriate times?

14. **CONFLICT HANDLING - ASSERTIVENESS.**

    Do you shy away from conflict? Are you very confrontational with conflict? Do you view conflict as a way to find a winner and loser? Are you passive aggressive?

15. **INTERDEPENDENCE.**

    How much do you depend on others? Too much, too little? Do you have a healthy attitude about working with others and working alone? How effective are you working with others?

16. **REFLECTIVE LEARNING.**

How honest are you with yourself about how you feel?
How do you feel communicating this to others?

Improving your Emotional Intelligence

After reflecting and being honest with yourself answering these questions you may see your strengths and weaknesses and you can devise practices and new habits that you can focus on to improve each area as needed. When you combine this with the Gamma Brain Technique and the Emotional Balance Technique your emotional intelligence will move to a new level.

> **MAXIMISE YOUR ENERGY, RESILIENCE AND PERFORMANCE ACTION STEP 4:**
> Developing your emotional intelligence. Expand your self-awareness and self-management skills. Become more aware of how others are thinking and feeling and improve your ability to manage others with a new level of awareness.

We have covered the main aspects of mind, brain, and emotions. In Part 3 *Managing your Fuel* we look at the two physiological rules that guarantees increased physical energy, emotional balance and mental clarity.

■ ■ ■

Part 3

Managing Your Fuel

Chapter 7

How to Eat to Maximise Your Energy, Resilience and Performance

I N 2011 there were over 300,000 diet and nutrition books in print. How do you work out which is the 'right' way to eat when the nutritional industry is a multibillion dollar marketing machine full of contradictions and conflicting advice?

The two physiological rules you need to follow to maximise your physical energy, emotional balance and mental clarity

1. THROUGHOUT THE DAY MAINTAIN BALANCED LEVEL OF BLOOD SUGAR.

2. DO NOT EAT FOODS YOU ARE INTOLERANT TO.

We will address the first one first. You can have the most powerful beliefs programmed into your mind, you can be free of doubt and anxiety and full of confidence, you can be the most emotionally intelligent person on earth, but if your blood sugar is too low all that goes out the window and you move into primitive survival mode. Balancing your blood sugar is absolutely essential not only for optimal performance but also for optimal health. Let's see how we do it.

Eating Fat Doesn't Make you Fat

For years our dietary habits have been based on an outdated belief that eating fat makes you fat and that low fat diets are the way to lose weight and improve health. Logically you could say it makes sense, eat less fat and you lose body fat, but scientifically it doesn't work. Fat is not the bad boy we have been left to believe. In a landmark study by Professor Kekwick at the University of London, two groups of patients were put on a low 1000 calorie a day diet. The first group's 1000 calories consisted of 90% fat and the second group's consisted of 90% carbohydrate. What happened? The high fat group lost significant amounts of body fat and the carbohydrate group lost virtually none.

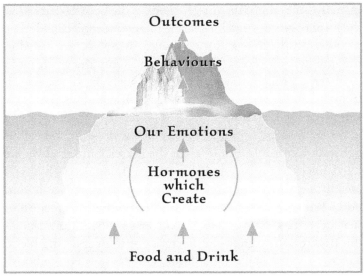

Fig 7.0: Each time we put food and drink into our mouth it creates specific hormones that control how we feel, think and act.

The Key to Permanent Fat Loss

The key to permanent fat loss and optimal health is the ratio of the macro nutrients; protein, carbohydrates and fat in each meal. Every time you eat, these macro nutrients create a specific hormonal response in the body. Hormones are messenger molecules that regulate virtually everything your body does. Hormones have a very large impact on how we feel and the quality of thoughts and actions. (**See Fig 7.0**) As Dr Barry Sears PhD points out in his bestselling book *The Zone*;

> *"Food is the most powerful drug you will ever encounter. Learning how to control hormonal responses to food is your passport to staying in the zone."*

The body and brain requires a constant supply of carbohydrate converted into glucose as its primary source of energy. Any carbohydrates not immediately used by the body are stored in the form of glycogen (a long string of glucose molecules linked together) in the liver and the muscles. The glycogen stored in the muscles is inaccessible to the brain. Only the glycogen in the liver is broken down and sent through the blood stream to maintain optimal brain function. A human body can only store about sixty to ninety grams of glycogen in the liver which is the equivalent to a small bowl of porridge or four slices of bread. Once glycogen levels in the muscles and the liver are filled any excess gets stored as fat. Even though carbohydrates are fat free, excess carbohydrate turns up as extra fat on your body! But there's worse to come. A high carbohydrate meal or snack creates a rapid rise in blood sugar which in turn signals the pancreas to secrete the hormone insulin into the blood stream to lower the levels of blood glucose to keep the body's energy in balance. Insulin is essentially a storage hormone which tells excess carbohydrate to store as fat as a survival mechanism in case of a future famine. So this means when we eat too much carbohydrate we are essentially sending a message to the body via the messenger insulin to 'store fat'.

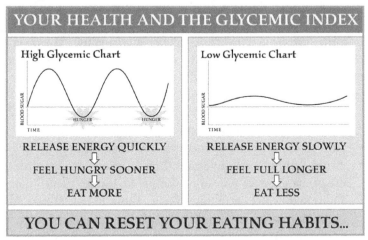

Fig 7.1:

As part of the survival mechanism insulin also tells the body not to release any stored fat. The bottom line is that excess carbohydrates make you fat and make sure you stay fat. Carbohydrates vary in the rate that they enter the bloodstream and the measure of this is called the glycemic index. The lower the glycemic (GI) index, the slower the rate into the bloodstream and the less insulin is produced. The higher the GI the faster the rate and the more insulin is produced. (See Fig 7.1)

When blood sugar levels spike too high, called hyperglycemia or drop too low, called hypoglycaemia our physical energy is unbalanced and we can become lethargic, emotionally erratic and irritable and our mental clarity and focus is diminished. Most people have experienced low blood sugar, most likely after eating a high carbohydrate meal at midday and feeling mentally fatigued and virtually asleep by 3pm.

Glucagon is the opposing hormone to insulin and increases blood sugar levels when they get too low. Whilst insulin is released by eating carbohydrate, glucagon is released by eating protein. Glucagon is your fat burning hormone. Think of insulin as a fat storage hormone and glucagon as a fat burning hormone. Now think of eating as a game. The object of the game is to eat meals and snacks that control the release of insulin and elevate glucagon. Do that and you win the game, gain energy and lost fat!

Guidelines for Keeping Blood Sugar Levels Stables

- Aim to eat three meals and two snacks per day.
- Avoid "white" carbohydrates; bread, pasta, rice, potatoes, crisps, sugary sweets and drinks including fruit juice. Don't eat white stuff unless you want to get fatter. All carbohydrates eaten should ideally be complex carbs; switch to brown rice, porridge, muesli made with oats,quinoa, millet, granary and seeded breads and buckwheat.
- All meals and snacks should contain protein along with the carbohydrates.
- Keep fruit to a maximum of 1 portion per day and when it is eaten add some protein with it to slow the release of sugar into the blood stream. For example, eat a small handful of nuts with your apple. The best fruit in terms of glycaemic content are berries; strawberries, raspberries, blackberries, blueberries, cherries and apples and pears.
- Keep your coffee and other high caffeine drinks to two a day. All stimulants including cigarettes cause the stimulation of the adrenal glands to release cortisol and adrenaline which cause the breakdown of glycogen into blood glucose. Insulin then acts to push this excess sugar into the cells as quickly as cells as quickly as possible. This is actually pushed into the cells of the abdominal region.

Stimulants cause weight gain in the abdominal region, even though you may not actually have consumed any sugar - just a cigarette and a cup of black coffee can make you fatter.

DO NOT EAT FOODS YOU ARE INTOLERANT TO.

A food intolerance is a negative stress reaction in the body to a food, beverage or food additive. Most people are intolerant or allergic to some type of food, drink or/and additive.

It is suggested that 80% of the population have an intolerance to wheat. This is due to the highly processed nature of wheat products on the market today. Commercially produced wheat products are stripped of the germ, bran, and majority of the fibre, vitamins, and minerals making it hard on our digestion, plus we eat too much of it. If you have a regular cloudy / foggy head then the first place to look would be a food intolerance.

You can spend hundreds of pounds on blood tests to see what your food intolerances are, but there is nothing more accurate than tuning into how you feel physically, mentally and emotionally after you have eaten. The easiest way to find this out is to use the Post Meal and Snack Test.

THE POST MEAL AND SNACK TEST
After one hour of eating your meals and snacks;
How do you feel physically?
Do you feel satisfied and have more energy than before eating or do you feel more tired?
If you feel more tired, then what you have eaten has taken more energy to metabolise and digest it than it is creating energy for you to use.

How do feel emotionally?
Do you feel calmer and more balanced than before eating or do you feel more anxious and unbalanced? If the latter then what you have eaten has not balanced your blood sugar or you have an intolerance to it.
How do you feel emotionally?
Do you feel calmer and more balanced than before eating or do you feel more anxious and unbalanced? If the latter then what you have eaten has not balanced your blood sugar.

If you are not physically, mentally and emotional feeling and functioning well after eating, then what you are eating is robbing your energy.

Do You Need to Take Supplements?

If you are eating lots of fresh veg and fruit from your own garden or a local organic farmers market every day and you have a relaxed low stress lifestyle, then maybe you can be healthy and a high performer without supplements. But who's doing that? Given the stress of our modern life, the poor quality of our food supply, and the high load of environmental toxins on our brains and bodies, we need to supplement to make sure we get the daily supply of the raw materials our bodies need to function. Remember your body is literally made of what you eat, drink and think!

As an absolute minimum take a high quality vitamin and mineral supplement and at least 2 grams of vitamin C a day.

**MAXIMISE YOUR ENERGY, RESILIENCE
AND PERFORMANCE ACTION STEP 5:**
Make balancing your blood sugar your nutritional priority.
From your next meal onwards start to view the composition
of each meal and snack as your energy source for your next
four to six hours. Choose low glycemic carbohydrates and
include protein with meal and snack.
Use the Post Meal and Snack Test every time you eat.
Take a high quality vitamin and mineral supplement and at
least 2 grams of vitamin C per day.

How Much Water do You Need to Drink?

Every single function of our bodies uses water. If you are
dehydrated, your blood becomes thicker (think of the
difference between water and jam) and it is slower to move
around the body and brain delivering the nutrients and
removing your waste products. 75% of your liver's job is to
remove toxins from the body and it cannot do that without
the appropriate amount of water. 2% dehydration creates up
to a 20% decline in your mental reasoning skills. Increasing
your dehydration alone can make a world of difference toyour
energy levels. A good estimate is to take your body weight in
pounds and divide that number by half. That gives you the
number of ounces of water per day that you need to drink. For
example, of you weigh 160 pounds, you should drink at least
80 ounces of water per day. If you exercise, you should drink
another eight ounce glass of water for every 20 minutes you
are active. If you drink alcohol, you should drink at least an
equal amount of water. When you are traveling on an airplane,
it is good to drink eight ounces of water for every hour you are
on board the plane. If you live in an arid climate, you should
add another two servings per day. As you can see, your daily
need for water can add up to quite a lot.

The most reliable way to check whether you're drinking enough is to look at the colour of your urine. It should be a light straw colour. If it's dark or strong-smelling, you're dehydrated. (This doesn't apply to your first pee of the morning, when you've been without a drink for some hours.)

**MAXIMISE YOUR ENERGY, RESILIENCE
AND PERFORMANCE ACTION STEP 6:**
Take our body weight in pounds and divide that number in half. That gives you the minimum number of ounces of water per day that you need to drink.

Go to my blog on **www.GammaMindset.com** and read the articles: "Essential Fatty Acids – Nutrition for Peak Performance", "Supplements for Optimal Health and Peak Performance" and "Food Intolerance; Food, Drink and Add-itives that May be Depleting your Energy and Ruining your Health".

In part 4; *Managing Your Body*, we explore the four key factors for increased physical energy, vibrant health, emotional balance and mental clarity.

■ ■ ■

Part 4

Managing Your Body

Chapter 8

Understanding your Body's Rhythms to Maximise Your Energy, Resilience and Performance

YOUR PHYSICAL ENERGY is the foundation for all your mental and emotional energy. The foundation for physical energy is sleep.

NOTHING HAS MORE INFLUENCE ON YOUR EVERYDAY EFFECTIVENESS THAN THE SLEEP YOU HAD THE NIGHT BEFORE.

Known as the leading expert in sleep research Dr William Dement from Stanford University in the USA, says that sleep may well be more critical to our wellbeing than diet, exercise and hereditary factors.

Q: How many hours sleep on average do you get each night?
Q: How many hours sleep do you think is best for optimal energy?

When researchers test subjects in an environment without clocks, 95% of them sleep between seven to eight hours a night. We cannot function optimally on any less yet many of us believe we can and often cut sleep by getting up early or going to bed late so we can get 'more done'. Dr Nick Baylis, author of *Learning from Wonderful Lives*, tells us

"We need at least eight hours sleep in every 24 hour period and we should ensure we get them. Pressures of modern life tempt many of us to cut back on our sleep, but that's a false economy since our efficiency drops rapidly if we don't get enough sleep. The stark fact is that most of us probably get about two hours less sleep per day than our grandparents."

If we cut our usual sleeping pattern by two hours a night for a week our mental performance becomes as inefficient as someone who is twice over the drink-driving limit. If we miss a full night's sleep our immune system drops by about 25%. Lack of sleep is also associated with obesity, digestive problems and triggering migraines. Based on my findings of asking thousands of people in organisations, the average amount of sleep people get is six and a half hours per night. We can actually tell ourselves stories that we do not need seven to eight hours and that we can perform just as well on less, but all the research suggests otherwise. Often we do not recognise when we are sleep deprived and think that our lack of energy during the day is 'just how it is.' As another leading sleep researcher Dr Charles Czeisler from Harvard Medical School tells us

"Like a drunk, a person who is sleep-deprived has no idea how functionally impaired he or she truly is. Most of us have forgotten what it really feels like to be awake."

In a study of nearly 10,000 people, subjects who slept five hours a night were 60% more likely to be overweight and obese than those that slept seven or more. The Harvard Nurses' Health Study which followed 80,000 nurses over a twenty five year period found a strong correlation between a lack of sleep and a range of diseases such as breast cancer, colon cancer and colon cancer and heart disease. Nurses that averaged five to six hours a night were significantly more likely to develop heart disease than those who slept seven or more. The evidence is overwhelming that sleep deprivation is detrimental to every aspect of our lives. Charles Leadbeater from the *Centre for Confidence and Wellbeing* in Scotland tells us:

> "We are taking risks without knowing how to calculate the costs and benefits of our actions. Sleep is vital to brain devel-opment in children and remains vital to learning, emotion and memory in adults. A society which sees sleep as enforced downtime, a maintenance period to be minimized, is taking huge risks. Denying ourselves the sleep we need can dent our productivity, reduce the quality of our work and erode our creativity and innovation. This can be particularly damaging in an economy where creativity at work is just as important as the hours we put in. Meanwhile, back home, sleep deprivation makes for increased tension and strife, especially where both parents are working and have young children to look after."

If you are not getting enough sleep, you almost certainly need to go to bed earlier as getting up later is probably not an option.

MAXIMISE YOUR ENERGY, RESILIENCE AND PERFORMANCE ACTION STEP 7:
Decide that a minimum of seven hours sleep a night becomes the norm.

During the night we move through five stages of sleep from light sleep to deep sleep, back to light sleep and then we wake up. These cycles move in 90 minute periods. During the day we also fluctuate approximately every ninety minutes from higher from higher to lower alertness known as 'ultradian cycles.' Physiologically our bodies are telling us we need a renewal period every ninety minutes to optimise our energy output. Unfortunately most of us have become so conditioned to think we can maintain the same drive and focus throughout the day that we miss the signs our body is giving us to slow down and renew. Often when we feel tired, irritable, or find it hard to concentrate, we reach for a coffee or perhaps high glycemic food to help us 'push through'. The down side to this is an increase in the stress hormones such as cortisol and adrenaline being released into the body. We get the quick kick of energy but inevitably end up with more anxiety, mental cloudiness and a lack of effectiveness. Understanding your body's energy rhythms is perhaps one of the most important factors you can master. Working out when you are most alert and focused allows you to plan your work schedule to maximise productivity. Working on your more complex tasks can be scheduled when you are most alert and vibrant, whilst completing more basic simple tasks can be done on a renewal cycle. Renewal periods can be as simple as walking the stairs, going outside for some daylight and fresh air, washing your face or using the Gamma Brain Technique and Emotional Balance Technique. Your body especially wants a passive renewal period between 1pm and 3pm which is a great time to do your Gamma Brain Technique meditation.

MAXIMISE YOUR ENERGY, RESILIENCE AND PERFORMANCE ACTION STEP 8:
Add at least two renewal periods each day and make one of these between 1pm and 3pm (not counting lunch) which is when the body most craves rest. Use the Gamma Brain Technique 5-10 minute meditation at least once a day.

Stress Causes Adrenal Fatigue

No bigger than a walnut and weighing less than a grape, each of your two adrenal glands sits like a tiny pyramid on top of a kidney. Don't let their size fool you, these powerful little glands manufacture and secrete hormones that are essential for life, health and vitality. They modulate the functioning of every tissue, organ and gland in your body to maintain balance during stress and keep you alive. They also have important effects on the way you think and feel.

The main purpose of your adrenals is to enable your body to deal with stress from every possible source, ranging from injury and disease to work and relationship problems. They largely determine the energy of your body's responses to every change in your internal and external environment. Whether they signal attack, retreat or surrender, every cell responds accordingly, and you feel the results. It is through the actions of the adrenal hormones that your body is able to mobilise its resources to escape or fight off danger (stress) and survive.

In a more primitive society that would mean being able to run away quickly, fight or pursue an enemy or game, endure long periods of physical challenge and deprivation, and store up physical reserves when they are available. In modern society, these same responses are triggered by such circumstances as work deadlines, air pollution, family quarrels, financial problems, too little sleep, illness and overindulgence in or sensitivities to food, alcohol or drugs. If your adrenal function is low, as it is in adrenal fatigue, your body has difficulty responding and adapting properly to these stresses. This can lead to a variety of physical and psychological health problems that are themselves a further source of stress. Unfortunately adrenal fatigue is very common in today's fast paced world.

How do you know if your Adrenal Glands are Overworked or Fatigued?

- Tired for no reason?
- Feel apathetic or lethargic frequently?
- Having trouble getting up in the morning?
- Need coffee, stimulants, salty or sweet snacks to keep going?
- Feeling run down, worn out or stressed?
- Not recovering from colds and illness as quickly as you used to?
- Feeling anxious or depressed?
- Having difficulty with your memory or concentration?
- Putting on fat especially around the belly?
- Low libido?

If you answered "yes" to two or more of these questions, your adrenal glands are probably fatigued along with other organs of your body, like your gut, liver and kidneys.

I have coached many city executives who have driven their body into a state of chronic fatigue by 'burning out' their adrenals. Long working hours, poor nutrition and not resting and renewing energy sufficiently is a sure fire way to create adrenal fatigue.

Keeping your adrenals healthy is an absolute necessity to every aspect of your overall well-being and vitality. It is impossible to increase your energy and resilience when you have fatigued adrenals.

Here are 10 ways to give your adrenals and other organs a boost:

1. Take a high quality vitamin and mineral supplement and at least two grams of vitamin C per day.

2. Don't eat fast food or food with artificial sweeteners and additives in it. Usually loaded with neurotoxins (neurotoxins distort brain function) like monosodium glutamate (MSG) and aspartame. Fast food can cause your body to be in a constant state of stress after eating it, until the chemicals are detoxified from your system. Depending on the strength of your liver's detoxification systems that can be anywhere from a few hours to several days.

3. Reduce your caffeine intake. Caffeine stimulates the adrenal glands only to cause an energy crash later on. Try herbal teas instead. Peppermint tea is a natural pick-me-up that doesn't stimulate the adrenal glands.

4. Avoid sugar and refined wheat products. They cause your blood sugar to fluctuate rapidly, which in turn causes your adrenals to overreact.

5. Eat some protein at every meal to stabilise blood sugar and prevent strain on the adrenals. That doesn't necessarily mean meat. Some good vegetarian sources of protein include: legumes (beans), nuts, seeds, avocado, and quinoa (a nutritious whole grain).

6. Reduce your stress. Use the Emotional Balance Technique daily to eliminate psychological and emotional stressors from your mind and body. Use the Gamma Brain Technique Meditation daily.

7. Get at least 7 hours sleep at night. If possible, don't wake to a blaring alarm clock since the noise causes a flood of stress hormones to be released.

8. Avoid alcohol for a while. Alcohol is another stimulant and puts stress on the liver which in turns stresses the adrenals and makes them even more fatigued.

9. Find some time every day to have a good laugh. Laughter releases all the feel good, healing chemicals. Remember your body is designed to heal. When you remove the stress that is exactly what it does.

10. Get out of the office, away from your computer and get as much natural light on your body every day. We all know how good it feels to have the sun on our face. Without getting sunburn, every day focus on getting sunlight on your face. The health benefits of sunlight are enormous.

MAXIMISE YOUR ENERGY, RESILIENCE AND PERFORMANCE ACTION STEP 9:
Do whatever you can to reduce your physical, mental and emotional stress.

■ ■ ■

Exercise - Do you really have to,
and if so how much do you need to do?

How do you become more productive? Richard Branson paused and thought for a moment. A group of twenty sat with him awaiting his reply. The group were brainstorming ideas for his Virgin Unite Enterprise. The Virgin Group have more than 300 companies and more than 50,000 employees with revenues of over $25 billion per year. After a minute of pondering, he answered; *"Work Out"*.

He explained to his group that he had come to realise that working out regularly gave him at least 4 hours a day of productive time.

Five time Olympic speed skating champion and orthopaedic surgeon Dr Eric Heiden explains in his book; *Faster, Better, Stronger;*

> *"How much you move, affects your strength, your power, your balance, how you look, how you think, how well you withstand the high winds and showers of life and how long you will stand. Everyone needs concentrated doses of several kinds of movement to remain fully functional."*

It's obvious that the more sedentary we become the fewer calories we burn, the more weight we gain, we lose strength, endurance, flexibility and this can turn into a very unproductive low energy lifestyle. In an amazing study to test the effects of inactivity on overall health, researchers at the South Western Medical School in Dallas recruited six college students to literally spend the summer in bed. After just three weeks in bed the subjects experienced deterioration in cardiovascular fitness equivalent to twenty years of ageing. Use it or lose it indeed.

Physical exercise renews and boosts not only our physical energy, but simultaneously boosts our emotional and mental energy too. As you have seen the mind and body are one system and as Professor William Tiller explains in his ground breaking book Psychoenergetic Science;

> *"Every change in the human physiological state is accompanied by an appropriate change in the mental emotional state, conscious or unconscious, and conversely every change in the human mental emotional state, conscious or unconscious, is accompanied by an appropriate change in the physiological state."*

Every body position and posture we adopt has a mental and emotional state linked to it, as expressed humorously in this cartoon - see **Fig 9.0.**

Fig 9.0:

Exercise - The Facts

The health and energy benefits to exercise are immense and the good news is you do not have to do as much to reap these benefits as you may have been led to believe. There has been a belief in the exercise and fitness industry that to improve your cardiovascular health and fitness you need to exercise 3-5 times per week for a minimum of 20 minutes. This has been taught in thousands of colleges and fitness courses worldwide for years. In the 1990's I used to manage a health club and my team were all trained with this as the ideal prescription for cardiovascular health and fitness. Millions of people worldwide still use this format today. This prescription is based on research that was incorrectly interpreted. Dr Wong, a leading naturopathic doctor with a PhD in exercise physiology explains this:

"The true Dean of cardiovascular exercise and father of cardiac stress testing was a Scandinavian exercise physiologist named Karvonen. His definitive work in the 50's and 60's showed that the heart began getting stronger i.e. more conditioned, after a mere 7 to 8 minutes worth of work. The idea that 20 minutes or more is needed in order to attain cardiovascular conditioning came from a misreading of research carried out by Dr Tom Cureton, Jr. Ph.D. another giant in exercise science. That research found that the plaque in the arteries began to be worn down, and so the lipids (fats) therein started to be used as fuel at around the 16 to 20 minute mark of aerobic exercise. The research did not mean that the heart did not condition before 16-20 minutes. Many non-experts however in the exercise field i.e. medical doctors, personal trainers and television stars (with workout videos to sell), understood it to mean just that" Dr Wong goes onto say *"Do cardiovascular work - minimum 8 minutes, top off at 24 minutes, no more than 3 times a week – period."*

Now of course if you are already an avid exerciser then you will probably be doing much more than this, but if you are not, then enjoy the fact you do not have to do much to gain great health benefits.

Easy Ways to get Fitter

In a study of 15,000 same sex twins the sibling who exercised regularly had a 55% lower risk of early death compared to the twin who did not. Interestingly the amount of exercise was very little – a brisk walking pace, six times a month for thirty minutes, totalling only three hours per month. The conclusion of a study published in *The Journal of the American Medical Association; "Exercise acts like a vaccine on the immune system."* In a meta-analysis of over one hundred studies on exercise in 2004 by researchers in London they concluded that

> *"Exercise improves mental health and well-being, reduces depression and anxiety and enhances cognitive functioning."*

In another study at Duke University in the USA researchers found that vigorous exercise for 30-45 minutes three times per week was more effective than anti-depressant drugs in reducing the symptoms of depression.

Exercise has to become a lifestyle and as necessary as brushing your teeth. However to make it become part of your lifestyle you have to find something you enjoy doing. From today choose some form of exercise even if as a minimum is a vigorous walk for at least 10 minutes per day. What things could you do at work that would increase your movement and physical activity? For example, a twelve week study on the effects of stair climbing on health and fitness showed very beneficial results. There were 69 participants who had what the researchers described as a sedentary lifestyle. Over the 12 weeks of the study, the volunteers, who were hospital employees at the university, were asked to use the stairs exclusively at work instead of taking the lift. On average, the number of flights of stairs - classed as climbing up or down one storey - rose from 5 per day to 23 per day. After the three months of the trial, tests showed the volunteers had better lung capacity, blood pressure and cholesterol measurements. Their weight, body fat and waist measurements also dropped, and their capacity for doing aerobic exercise improved. So you don't have to join a gym or be some super athlete to achieve huge health and energy benefits.

One of the most beneficial forms of exercise is resistance training, and the best form of resistance training is weight training. Why is this so good? Because weight training is the best way to deal with, and even to reverse, the effect of biological ageing. Studies have shown that after six months of weight training just three times per week for twenty minutes each session, the indicators of biological ageing were reduced by twelve years! When most people think of weight training, they think of the stereotypical image of bodybuilders straining to build huge muscles. Unless you plan on spending hours in the gym and consuming anabolic steroids and growth hormone this is just not going to happen. The truth is that the health benefits of weight training go way beyond any other form of exercise. Here is a short list of some of the benefits of weight training (and of certain types of resistance training):

- Strengthens your muscles, tendons and ligaments, helping you achieve a strong, balanced posture and an increase in strength and endurance for everyday tasks.
- Raises your basal metabolic rate by as much as 15%, which causes you to burn more calories throughout the

day well after your exercise is done and even while you're sleeping. Weight training can make your body burn up to 300 additional calories a day (for someone who normally burns 2000 calories per day), so over time, it can lead to significant fat loss.

- Strengthens your bones, reducing your risk of developing osteoporosis.
- Decreases your resting blood pressure.
- Improves your balance and co-ordination.
- Increases your blood level of HDL cholesterol (the good type).
- Enhances immune system functioning.

In a nutshell weight or resistance training helps keep you youthful. In July 2008 a major study was published in the British Medical Journal. The researchers followed 8762 American men aged between twenty to sixty years for 19 years. At the start of study the men received a physical exam, a strength test and a cardiovascular test. Men with poor health or poor health history were removed from the study at the start. Over the 19 years 503 men died. But here's the kicker - overall there were 50% more deaths in the weakest third of the men, than in the middle or upper third. When the researchers looked at the deaths from cardiovascular disease and cancer the weakest men died earliest.

Strength training keeps you youthful and not only prolongs your life but prolongs the quality of your life. Having had a previous career in the health and fitness industry, I know only too well that many people start an exercise program with high enthusiasm, only to lose interest and discipline after a while. This is usually due to beliefs, learned in our younger years, that exercise is hard work and boring. This is a belief that can be changed. In addition, many of us are overscheduled, and we think we cannot possibly undertake one more activity. However, if you examine your life, you will find that you usually make time for what is important to you. Changing your belief structure can make exercise an enjoyable part of your life. Let's say your goal is to improve your health, fitness and vitality, so you consider joining a gym, doing yoga or jogging. When you think of exercise, your immediate emotional reaction reveals the essence of your beliefs about the situation. Perhaps your immediate feelings include anxiety, boredom or even fear. These feelings could be driven by a set of beliefs that sound like the following inner self-talk:

> I've never been sporty or liked exercise.
> Exercise is hard work and draining.
> I'm too old for hard workouts.
> I don't have the time to exercise, just thinking about adding one more thing to my day drains me.

These beliefs belie a likely outcome – you won't be exercising anytime soon. Or, if you do join the gym in that initial burst of surface enthusiasm, soon your core beliefs will have you finding reasons why perhaps the sofa and TV remote control may seem a better option.

How might the situation be different if the following were your true, spontaneous, unmediated inner self-talk?

■ ■ ■

Exercise increases my energy.
Exercise improves my health.
A healthy body is a healthy mind.
Exercise is a great way to relieve stress.
Exercise keeps me youthful.

Exercise creates more energy and with more energy you are more resilient and can perform better. So from today decide what type of exercise is going to become part of your lifestyle. Here are some suggestions:

Power Walking for at least 10 minutes a day
Taking the stairs instead of the lifts
Yoga
Running
Weight Training
Exercise Classes
Dancing
Cycling
Martial Arts
Swimming
What is it to be?

MAXIMISE YOUR ENERGY, RESILIENCE AND PERFORMANCE ACTION STEP 10:
Start an exercise plan that you enjoy and make it part of your lifestyle.

We conclude this book by reviewing the ***10 steps to Maximise your Energy, Resilience and Performance*** and you can take ***the 30 day challenge***.

Chapter 9

The 10 Steps to Maximise Your Energy, Resilience and Performance

STEP 1. Every day in every conversation be consciously aware. Use the STOP model. Be as present and in the moment as you can. Make your choices and responses from a conscious place.

STEP 2. • Every day use the Gamma Brain Technique to integrate new empowering beliefs into your subconscious mind.
• Use the technique at key times throughout the day to achieve a super focused mind state or solve problems.
• Use the technique as a 5-10 minutes rest and renewal meditation at least once a day, ideally mid-afternoon when your body most craves rest.

STEP 3. Clear your emotional stressors one at a time. Use the Emotional Balance Technique as often as required until you feel emotionally clear and balanced and you are reacting less and less from your autopilot emotional brain.

STEP 4. Develop your emotional intelligence. Expand your self-awareness, self-management and awareness of management of others at every opportunity.

STEP 5. Make balancing your blood sugar your nutritional priority. From your next meal onwards start to view the composition of each meal and snack as your energy source for your next four to six hours. Choose low glycemic carbohydrates and include protein in every meal and snack. Use the post meal/snack test with everything you eat.

STEP 6. Take your body weight in pounds and divide that number in half. That gives you the minimum number of ounces of water per day that you need to drink.

STEP 7. Decide that a minimum of seven hours sleep a night becomes the norm.

STEP 8. Have at least two rest and renewal periods each day and make one of these between 1pm and 3pm which is when the body most craves rest (not counting lunch). Use the 5-10 minute Gamma Brain Technique meditation as one of your renewal periods.

STEP 9. Do whatever you can to reduce your physical, mental and emotional stress.

STEP 10. Start an exercise plan that you enjoy and make it part of your lifestyle.

TAKE ACTION NOW:

Get your free video training course
www.ChrisWaltonUK.com

Sign up for your Free Video Training Course at
www.ChrisWaltonUK.com

Chris@ChrisWaltonUK.com
+44 0207 751 9794

■ ■ ■

Appendix

Belief
Statements

Turning Stress into Success

1. I respond to changes calmly and creatively.
2. I am centred and energised by changes in my life.
3. I respond to work deadlines calmly and creatively.
4. I am compassionate and understanding even during times of conflict with others.
5. I make the best out of situations, even when I can't change them.
6. I naturally focus on the positive solutions to negative situations.
7. I typically see challenges in my life as opportunities for creative problem solving.
8. I choose healthy and nutritious foods to fuel my body.
9. I take the necessary risks to succeed in life.
10. I face demands head on and take direct action to meet them.
11. I am clear about my priorities and stay consistently focused in accomplishing them.
12. I am comfortable asking others for help when I need it.
13. I am comfortable sharing my thoughts and feelings with others.
14. I know the difference between what is urgent and what is important.
15. I am patient with myself even when I don't accomplish everything I had planned.
16. I adapt to new challenges and situations easily and naturally.
17. I am a creative problem solver in situations that are new to me.
18. I thrive and am creative in a changing environment.
19. I am clear about what is important and I stay focussed on my real priorities.
20. I organise my time so that I am optimally effective.

Effective Communication

1. I communicate my skills, knowledge and experience with clarity and confidence.
2. I listen to what others have to say with genuine interest.
3. I am a powerful and effective communicator.
4. I seek first to understand others before trying to be understood.
5. I am open and honest in my communication.
6. I let people finish talking without interrupting.
7. My opinions are as valid as anyone else's.
8. I understand we all filter the world differently.
9. It is easy for me to agree to disagree.
10. It is okay for others to disagree with me.
11. I find it easy to give compliments to others.
12. I find it easy to receive compliments from others.
13. I trust my ability to say the right thing at the right time.
14. I give feedback with empathy and fairness.
15. I trust my ability to communicate effectively.
16. I can admit when I am wrong.
17. I am comfortable speaking to large groups of people.
18. People like to be around me.
19. I naturally look for the good in other people.
20. I remain relaxed and calm when speaking to groups of people.

Self Esteem and Confidence

1. I deeply appreciate and accept myself just the way I am.
2. I am valuable as a person even when I make mistakes.
3. I do the best I can and let the rest go.
4. I naturally expect the best from myself and others.
5. I am an optimistic person.
6. What I do makes a difference.
7. I trust my ability to successfully meet life's challenges.

8. I am a winner personally and professionally.
9. I attract friends and colleagues that are supportive and caring.
10. I deserve supportive relationships in my life.
11. I say what I mean and I mean what I say.
12. It is okay for others to disagree with me.
13. It is okay for me to disagree with others.
14. I trust my body to let me know when it needs a break.
15. I am the one who has the power to decide how I feel moment to moment.
16. I deeply accept and appreciate myself.
17. I forgive myself for all my imperfect thoughts and actions past, present and future.
18. I love myself unconditionally.
19. I am worthy of being loved.
20. I love all parts of my body.
21. I accept my imperfections as opportunities to learn valuable lessons in my life.
22. I deserve to be happy.
23. I deserve the very best life has to offer.
24. I deserve to love myself.
25. I deserve to be loved by (input a specific name here or simply say 'by others').
26. I deserve to love (input a specific name here or simply say 'others').
27. I am patient and curious when others criticise me.
28. I am confident and self-assured about who I am.
29. I am confident and self-assured about my life.
30. I am the best me I can be in each moment.
31. I have faith and confidence in my future.
32. I trust myself.
33. I take responsibility for my own well-being.

34. I am proud of who I am.
35. I am at peace with myself now.

The Seven Habits of HIghly Effective People

BE PROACTIVE
1. I am proactive and in charge of my own life.
2. I make decisions and carry them through.

BEGIN WITH THE END IN MIND
1. I consistently look for and expect the best from myself and others.
2. I have a clear sense of purpose in my life.

PUT FIRST THINGS FIRST
1. I organise and execute my life around priorities.
2. I naturally recognise and respond to what is important in my life rather than what is urgent.

THINK WIN / WIN
1. I genuinely seek mutual benefit in all my relationships, both personal and professional.
2 My thoughts and actions continuously express my Win/Win attitude.
3. I actively listen to and enthusiastically seek to understand points of view other than my own.

SEEK FIRST TO UNDERSTAND, THEN TO BE UNDERSTOOD
1. I seek to understand others before stating my own point of view.
2. I do my best to understand others emotionally as well as intellectually.

SYNERGISE
1. I value the difference in myself and others.
2. I build on the strengths in myself and others.
3. I trust the process of synergy in my life.

SHARPEN THE SAW
1. I energise my body with the good nutrition and exercise.
2. Sleep and rest energise my body.

Peak Sales Performance
1. I have pride in myself as a salesperson.
2. I am proud of the ways in which I can help my customers.
3. My integrity is the real power behind successful selling.
4. My power of integrity helps me to make bigger and more profitable sales.
5. I am worth the money I receive.
6. It is okay for me to want money and I do want it.
7. I enjoy making lots of money.
8. I have what it takes, and I am willing to do what it takes, to create my life the way I want it.
9. I feel relaxed and confident when I ask for business and for payment.
10. I am centred and energised by changes in my life.
11. It is okay to have more money than I need.
12. I am ready, willing and able, to take the necessary risks to meet my sales goals.
13. I take 100% responsibility for my actions.
14. I am comfortable with my successes and I know who I am around other successful people.
15. When I hear "no" from a customer or prospect, it is a rejection of the sales message, not of me.
16. I learn from my mistakes as well as my successes.

Exceptional Leadership

1. I am confident and powerful.
2. I achieve what I set out to do.
3. I listen with the intent to understand.
4. I am worthy of courtesy and respect.
5. I am compassionate and understanding.
6. I am trustworthy.
7. I am honest with myself and others.
8. I radiate enthusiasm and integrity.
9. I am willing to share power with others.
10. I am willing to make tough choices.
11. I remain calm and centered when having difficult conversations.
12. I believe in my ability to lead others.
13. I treat others with dignity and respect.
14. I am passionate about my work.
15. I am a good problem solver.
16. I am disciplined and focused.
17. I am flexible and creative in times of change and uncertainty.

Relationships

1. It is easy for me to give love to (input the name of a specific person or simply say 'others').
2. It is easy for me to receive love from (input the name of a specific person or simply say 'others').
3. I am worthy of an intimate, passionate, romantic relationship.
4. I am willing to risk loving and being loved.
5. It is easy and natural for me to express my sexuality in a relationship.
6. I am able to maintain my individuality in my relationship (with could name a specific person).

7. I release my relationship with (input a specific name) when it's time to let go.
8. It is important for me to set boundaries in my relationships, and I do.
9. It is important for me to get my needs met in a relationship.
10. I am able to experience freedom in a relationship.
11. It is okay for my partner (input a specific name) to disagree with me.
12. I accept that my relationships change.
13. It is okay for me to express my truth in a relationship.
14. I allow others to grow and change or to stay as they are in a relationship.
15. I am true to my feelings in a relationship.
16. I allow myself to learn from others as they learn from me.
17. I allow myself to be sensitive and vulnerable in a relationship.
18. I allow others to learn their own lessons in a relationship.
19. I learn from my past relationships and create even better ones in the future.
20. I take full responsibility for my actions in my relationships.

Wealth

1. I trust myself to manage money honestly and sensibly.
2. Every part of me is ready, willing and able to create lots of money now.
3. I am calm and self-assured when I have money.
4. I am calm and self-assured when I do not have money.
5. I deserve to have all the money I need.
6. My worth as a person and my financial worth are two different things.
7. It is okay for me to want money.

8. I enjoy making lots of money.
9. I am confident and self-assured when I ask for business and for payment.
10. I receive and accept money with love and gratitude.
11. It is okay to have more money than I need.
12. It is okay for me to have more money than other people.
13. It is okay for me to make mistakes with money.
14. It is safe and appropriate for me to create lots of money.
15. Money is a wonderful tool that I use to create possibility for myself and others.
16. My world is a friendly place and willingly provides whatever I need.
17. I can make all the money I need doing a job that I love.
18. Money is another manifestation of energy.

Body and Health

1. It is my natural birth right to be happy and healthy.
2. My mind and body heals itself, naturally and quickly.
3. I choose to live a healthy and vibrant life.
4. I accept optimal health as a natural part of my life.
5. I have all the energy and focus I need to accomplish my goals and to fulfil my desires.
6. It is safe for me to be slim and healthy.
7. It is easy and fun for me to be slim and healthy.
8. It is safe and appropriate to change the shape and weight of my body.
9. I can be everything I want to be as a healthy and fit person.
10. I love and accept my body as it is and as it changes.
11. I see beauty in all parts of my body.
12. I enjoy taking care of myself physically, mentally and emotionally.

Self-Empowerment and Professional Development

1. I trust the decisions I make.
2. I trust the divine guidance I am receiving.
3. I acknowledge my abilities and responsibility to make a positive difference in the world.
4. I proactively embrace the opportunities that come with change.
5. I now take the initiative to create my life the way that I want it.
6. I speak my personal truths with commitment and wisdom.
7. I learn and grow from my mistakes.
8. I use time efficiently and creatively and I experience having all the time I need.
9. My fears give me lessons that lead me to wisdom and power.
10. I take the risks necessary to live my life openly and honestly.
11. I experience the potential in myself and others in all my life experiences.
12. I do what I love and love what I do.
13. I am assertive in meeting my own needs.
14. I take action on my projects with inspiration and energy.
15. I now live life to the fullest.

■ ■ ▮

About the Author

Chris is an internationally recognised performance psychologist and consciousness researcher. He has trained world champion athletes and corporate executives to achieve peak performance. He teaches 'Resilience and Mental Fitness' on the MBA programme at the University of Westminster Business School and works in 1:1 private practice in London. He is also the author of the best-selling book:

The Gamma Mindset
Create the Peak Brain State and Eliminate
Subconscious Limiting Beliefs, Anxiety, Fear and Doubt in just
90 Seconds! And Awaken the Next Stage of Your Potential
to Create the Future You Want

www.ChrisWaltonUK.com
Chris@ChrisWaltonUK.com

CPSIA information can be obtained
at www.ICGtesting.com
Printed in the USA
LVHW03s0033111018
593106LV00001B/60/P

9 780956 552716